FREEDOMCIVICS®
FOUNDATIONS OF AMERICAN GOVERNMENT

COLLEGE EDITION

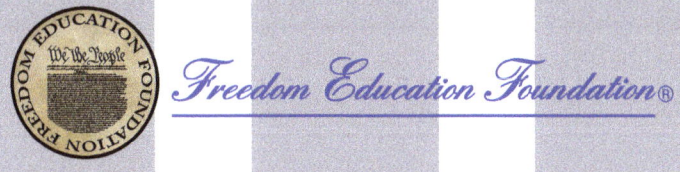

FREEDOMCIVICS®
FOUNDATIONS OF AMERICAN GOVERNMENT
COLLEGE EDITION

Copyright 2024 Freedom Education Foundation, Inc.

First edition of the high school versions were published in 2021.

Post Office Box 6
Bellevue, WA 98009

All Rights Reserved

Published by Freedom Education Foundation, Inc.
ISBN 9-798218-432492

Permission is hereby granted to quote short selections from FreedomCivics® if properly attributed to FreedomCivics® and the Freedom Education Foundation.

PREFACE

We want to share the blessings of freedom by distributing historically accurate curricula about the founding of the United States of America. We will not be content to simply offer educational resources. Our mission is to work tirelessly to get our 20-session civics course about the Founding Documents and free enterprise adopted in private, home, and public schools across America. We will be relentless in this effort, modeling the commitment of the Founders.

Watch for our announcement of the FreedomCivics online training platform. This world-class digital version (based on the printed textbooks) will be accessible through laptops, tablets, and mobile devices. It will teach and engage students using video along with many interactive quizzes available during or after class. To receive updates about this software version and updates about our curriculum and other educational programs, send your name and contact information (including mailing address) to newsletter@freedomeducation.org. To learn about our plans to improve civics education through FreedomCivics and efforts at the state level, send an email to legislation@freedomeducation.org.

Note that we plan to produce other curricula, possibly on *The Federalist*, the inaugural addresses of the first four presidents, the Magna Carta, and other documents of freedom. We are interested in your suggestions, whether about what we have already produced or curricula you would like us to develop. Please send your ideas by mail to FEF, P.O. Box 6, Bellevue, Washington 98009. Or email curriculum@freedomeducation.org.

Our mission at the Freedom Education Foundation is to research, develop and disseminate accurate history and civics curriculum. We focus on the founding documents of the United States and the principles of the Founders that resulted in the most freedom and greatest nation in the history of the world.

Craig W. Rhyne

Craig W. Rhyne, President

www.FreedomCivics.org

FreedomCivics® Contents

Acknowledgments		vi
Overview of FreedomCivics®		vii
Lesson 1	The Spirit of the American Revolution: Historical Foundations	1
Lesson 2	The First Colonies: Advancing Liberty in the New World	9
Lesson 3	The Enlightenment and Foundations of American Government	19
Lesson 4	Declaration of Independence and the Causes of Revolution	27
	Map of the Revolutionary War Battles	32
	Declaration of Independence, full text	34
Lesson 5	Articles of Confederation	39
	Articles of Confederation and Perpetual Union, full text	46
Lesson 6	Northwest Ordinance of 1787	53
	Map of the Northwest Territory in 1787 Showing Future States	54
	Northwest Ordinance of 1787, full text	61
Lesson 7	Constitutional Convention of 1787	67
	Constitution of the United States of America, full text	75
Lesson 8	U.S. Constitution Preamble and Article I. Legislative Branch	85
	How Does a Bill Become a Law?	92
Lesson 9	U.S. Constitution, Article II. Executive Branch	93
Lesson 10	U.S. Constitution, Articles III–VII. Judicial Branch and Implementation of the Constitution	99
Lesson 11	Review of the U.S. Constitution	105
Lesson 12	Ratification Debates	111
	The Federalist Number 10, full text	117
	The Federalist Number 51, full text	121

Lesson 13	Bill of Rights Amendments I–VIII	**125**
	Amendments I–X, full text	**131**
Lesson 14	Bill of Rights Amendments IX and X and Federalism	**133**
Lesson 15	Amendments XI–XVII, full text	**139**
Lesson 16	Amendments XVIII–XXVII, full text	**145**
Lesson 17	Upholding the Constitution and Protecting Civil Rights	**153**
Lesson 18	Final Review, Part One	**165**
Lesson 19	Final Review, Part Two, and the Duties of a Good Citizen	**171**
INDEX		**176**
Appendix I	Resources	**181**

FREEDOMCIVICS®

www.FreedomCivics.org

Acknowledgments

The Founders learned from history the need to limit the power of government, leading to the Declaration of Independence, the Revolutionary War, and the Constitution. Without exaggeration, their roots in Judeo-Christian law produced an exceptional nation, advancing human rights and progress as never before.

FEF wishes to express its gratitude and profound recognition to the principal developers and writers Richard Calkins and Craig Rhyne. We also thank Denise Rhyne for her guidance, as well as Karen Olson and Dr. Clark Summers for their excellent writing and editing work. Further, we thank the many teachers and parents who provided feedback about the sessions.

Special thanks to the FEF Board of Governors: Suzanne Burke, Richard Calkins, Richard Patten, Craig Rhyne, Clark Summers, PhD, and Frederic Weiss. They provided excellent ideas, oversight of the curriculum development, and financial support.

With deep appreciation but also great sadness, we honor the memory of Al Gibson, one of three charter members of FEF, who passed away in January 2022. One of his greatest causes was educating America's youth about the founding of the United States, especially about the Declaration of Independence, Articles of Confederation, Northwest Ordinance of 1787, and U.S. Constitution. Al generously supported FEF in developing and promoting the FreedomCivics course. We thank his widow Gloria and their daughter Nicole for encouraging the work of FEF in his honor.

Additionally, we appreciate the encouragement and advice from members of the FEF Board of Advisors: Dennis D. Case, Bruce K. Chapman, Glenn M. Dobbs, George A. Duff, James R. Medley, Stephen Moore, Jeff Morton, Hon. Richard B. Sanders, Esq., Howard Segermark, Larry J. Sundquist, Walter E. Williams, PhD (1936–2020), and Peter W. Wood, PhD.

Donations from many people over the years have made FreedomCivics possible. We are especially grateful for very generous contributions from John and Polly Addison, Suzanne Burke, Richard and Elizabeth Calkins, Clark and Mary Crawford, Al and Gloria Gibson, George and Karolyn Ghosn, Clyde and Rena Holland, Michael and Carol Gregg, Jim and Mary Kaye Johnston, Jack McMillan, Chet Stewart, Larry and Diane Sundquist, Betty Ward, Fred and Martha Weiss, and anonymous donors.

We also want to thank Christine Horner of Open Book Design and Jim Bowers and Leslie Welch-Piel at Precision Press for their fine work.

FEF is also very pleased that Shirley Crook, the widow of the renowned artist Don Crook, has allowed FEF to use his *Making of a Nation* painting on the covers of the FreedomCivics workbooks. The painting features the Declaration of Independence with seven of the Founders seated or standing in miniature with thirteen books (top left), representing the Thirteen Colonies.

Freedom Education Foundation

www.FreedomCivics.org

Overview of FreedomCivics®

FreedomCivics was developed by a team of teachers and historians for the Freedom Education Foundation (FEF). We are dedicated to providing an accurate history of the founding of the United States of America, with a focus on the Declaration of Independence, the Articles of Confederation, the Northwest Ordinance of 1787, and the U.S. Constitution. The 20-session civics course includes history of the American colonies, the Revolutionary War, free enterprise, and a balanced portrayal of American history. It also addresses the efforts of the Founders and our forefathers to work for "a more perfect union." It concludes with examples of contemporary challenges to the Constitution and to encourage students to be good citizens and protect the rights it guarantees.

FEF publishes high school teacher and student texts, as well as college versions. The teacher and student texts are identical except the Teacher includes answers to discussion questions and additional resources.

We have prepared a test/discussion bank of 99 questions (with answers) that cover the material. They are available for free in either a digital format or physical copy by emailing info@freedomeducation.org. A digital format of the curriculum is also available.

Both workbooks contain the full text of the four Founding Documents, also known as the "Organic Laws" of the United States of America, as designated by federal law in 1958. The Bill of Rights and the following 17 amendments to protect our rights and correct previous injustices are included. FEF highly recommends that students read the Founding Documents in their entirety. This College Edition has been updated to include the full text of Federalist 10 and Federalist 51.

The FreedomCivics model is based on 50-minute classes, starting with a review of various principles and forms of government—from ancient history to the Enlightenment. Natural law is explained, as well as the thinking of the Founders that led them to create a republic based on liberty and consent of the governed. The principles of freedom, private property rights, and the rule of law are woven throughout the 20 sessions. The course includes more than 100 thought-provoking discussion questions. Suggested test questions can be provided upon request.

There are many ways the material in this course can be used, either using all the lessons or inserting some of the lessons in existing curriculum.

Differences of Opinion

Invitation to Teachers

The Freedom Education Foundation recognizes there are disagreements and varied opinions about our history and interpretations of the actions of the Founders. Because of this, we are very open to receiving feedback from teachers and students about the FreedomCivics course. We are keenly interested in continually improving the FreedomCivics course.

Please send your comments and suggestions to Freedom Education Foundation, Attn: Curriculum Development, P.O. Box 6, Bellevue, WA 98009. Or email suggested changes to curriculum@freedomeducation.org.

Lesson 1

The Spirit of the American Revolution: Historical Foundations

Happily for America, happily, we trust, for the whole human race, they pursued a new and more noble course. They accomplished a revolution which has no parallel in the annals of human society. They reared the fabrics of governments which have no model on the face of the globe. They formed the design of a great confederacy, which it is incumbent on their successors to improve and perpetuate.

James Madison, The Federalist No. 14

Compelling Question: What are the historical and cultural roots that led to the foundation of the United States of America?

Key Concepts

1. Great Britain's North American colonies were an expression of the cultural heritage of Western civilization, reflecting multiple, diverse influences.

2. A desire for religious freedom was the primary reason English Puritans came to America, and their values laid an important foundation for colonial American life.

3. Classical Greek and Roman cultures provided the foundations of government by citizen rule in the forms of democracies and republics.

4. English Parliamentary experience established the concept of the rule of law applying to all citizens, including limits on the authority of the king or queen.

The Founders' American Dream: A Nation of Free People

In the late 1700s, the Thirteen American Colonies were in turmoil. King George III of England ruled harshly and disrespected the colonists' rights as English citizens. American colonists known as **Patriots** opposed British **tyranny**. Although some Blacks and Native Americans were Loyalists, others fought on the side of the Patriots.

Some of the American colonies were settled by people seeking religious and economic freedom. For example, thousands of English Puritans left the Church of England because they believed it was insufficiently reformed, and they were abused because of their views. But America was the beneficiary because of their values of hard work, responsibility, honesty, and self-control.

Puritan attitudes of self-reliance, frugality, industry, and energy established a strong foundation for the success of the United States.

The Patriots longed for liberty. They believed in what is called "**natural law**"—that God created all people equal, that everyone has **natural rights** that no government can take away, and that governments' authority comes from the **consent of the governed**.

> ***Revolutionary idea:*** The opening words of the United States Constitution are "We the People." We citizens are the government. The government gets all its authority from us. For thousands of years, no other nation had been founded on the idea that the people, not the ruler, are in charge of the government.

Although women, slaves, and men who didn't own land lacked full rights of citizenship during the Revolutionary War and at the founding of our nation, most of our Founders supported natural rights for everyone. They included in the Constitution a process so that future generations could amend (change) it.

These principles inspired the Patriots to revolt against Great Britain. They also were the basis for the Declaration of Independence, the Articles of Confederation, the Northwest Ordinance of 1787, and the U.S. Constitution. In this course, students will learn about the big ideas in these Organic Laws that advanced the cause of freedom and limited the powers of government. No matter what our background, we have all benefited from the system of government the Founders gave us.

History That Inspired a Revolution and the Founding of Our Nation

The big ideas they learned from history led to the Revolutionary War, shaped the founding of our exceptional nation, and advanced human rights and progress as never before.

These leaders had a classical education. They read the Bible, studied ancient Greek and Roman scholars, and were thoroughly familiar with English history and law. They were philosophers and historians who studied various types of government—current and past. They also were practical men. They wanted to know what worked and what didn't. Which systems of government ended in tyranny, and which provided some measure of freedom, peace, and prosperity? Here's a summary of what they and many American colonists knew.

Judeo-Christian Law. Familiarity with Judeo-Christian **civic** and moral law as written in the Bible was widespread in colonial America. Many of the colonists who fled England because of religious persecution compared their plight to the Israelites who fled slavery in Egypt. They found constitutional principles of separation of powers, checks and balances, limited government, due process, and unbiased justice in the Hebrew books of law.

Included are commandments against murder, physically harming people, stealing their private property, and oppression by rulers. The Constitution can be understood more fully by realizing the importance of these Judeo-Christian laws at the time our nation was founded. But, of course, they weren't the only influence.

Ancient Greek Democracy. The Founders studied ancient Greek history and philosophy. The Greeks formed many independent city-states with different forms of government. **Democracy** was born in the city-state of Athens in 507 BC and existed for many years. Citizens of Athens participated in "direct democracy" by meeting in local assemblies, debating issues, and voting. A simple majority determined how the city-state would operate. Citizens highly valued their freedom to speak and right to vote. But direct democracy often resulted in instability and wars.

The Founders recognized the benefits of freedom and self-determination under Athenian democracy. But they also saw the pitfalls. They rejected direct democracy because of its tendency toward mob rule, often descending into **anarchy**, and trampling on the rights of those in the minority.

The word *democracy* is not found in the U.S. Constitution or any state constitution, yet most people think the United States is a democracy. In fact, the U.S. is a **constitutional republic**, and the Founders spoke against democracy as a form of government because the majority can vote away individual rights of those in the minority and impose group rights by force. (See Session 7.)

Roman Republic. The Republic (509–27 BC) wasn't a direct democracy like Athens. Each year Roman citizens elected two chief officials. Usually, they were generals who led armies to war. The Republic was governed by the Assemblies and the Senate—similar to the **bicameral** Congress with its U.S. House of Representatives and the Senate. Citizens directly elected Assembly members to approve laws. At first, the Senate was an **aristocracy** and the dominant branch of the government. Senators managed the government and foreign policy and advised the chief officials. The Senate often overturned the Assemblies' decisions. This weakened the citizens' direct voice in how the government operated. Eventually, the Roman Republic was replaced by the Roman Empire, which was ruled by a dictator—the emperor. The Senate's influence and power weakened, and it finally dissolved.

The most important Roman politician and writer during this time was the brilliant and wise Cicero. He wrote two classic books based on natural law. He believed that there was a god who created the universe and natural law. He also believed that people are able to reason correctly, form **civil** governments, and rule justly.

The Founders agreed with Cicero's principles of natural law. The term "Laws of Nature and Nature's God" appears in the Declaration of Independence and in their writings. Our constitutional system is based on natural law (as defined by Sir William Blackstone, an English judge and author of *Commentaries on the Laws of England*). We see it in the ideals of **inalienable** rights, consent of the governed, limited government, checks and balances, and a republican **federal** system.

English History and Law. The Founders studied the people's political rights in England that developed over centuries. In fact, this knowledge contributed to the colonists' decision to revolt against England because King George III was violating their natural rights as English citizens.

    a. **Magna Carta.** One of the most significant advances in political rights was the Magna Carta, the first written constitution. King John had deprived the nobles of their rights as Englishmen and imposed heavy taxes to pay for his failed policies. So, when civil war broke out, the barons forced him to sign the Magna Carta in 1215. This great charter listed and protected the rights of free Englishmen, restricted the power of the **monarchy**, and established the principle that no person, including the monarch, was above the law.

    b. **Parliament.** The English Parliament advanced citizens' voices in the government. Parliament arose over time as a way to handle national issues. It was made up of the unelected House of Lords (the aristocracy) and the House of Commons elected by the people. English monarchs regularly went to war and had to find a way to pay for it. To raise taxes, they needed the permission of Parliament. This established the principle of no taxation without representation.

    The authority of Parliament and the rights of the English increased after three English Civil Wars and the Glorious Revolution of 1688. King James II ruled by tyranny, believing he was not accountable to the law or the people. The English overthrew him for disregarding English law and liberties. After being crowned king, William of Orange signed the English Bill of Rights in 1689. It limited the powers of rulers, laid out the powers of Parliament, and safeguarded individual rights. These rights included the power of Parliament (not the king or queen) to levy taxes, the right of members of Parliament to speak freely, and people's right to petition the monarch. The English Bill of Rights inspired the American colonists to demand their rights from the English government.

The Great Awakening. A Christian revival swept through the American colonies in the 1730s and 1740s. The English preacher George Whitefield and the American preacher Jonathan Edwards challenged the established church standards and old clergy throughout New England. Their preaching stirred the population, and Christianity grew dramatically. As a result, many colleges were founded, such as Princeton, Brown, Rutgers, and Dartmouth. Their preaching inspired a wave of missionary work in the colonies among Indians and black slaves. The most important effect of The Great Awakening was the sense of national unity that the colonists gained as a result. Most scholars say this was key in uniting the colonists to separate from Great Britain in the Revolutionary War.

A Nation Founded So We Could Have Life, Liberty, and Private Property

After studying all the types of government, the Founders decided that no current or past system was ideal. Leaving the country to anarchy certainly wasn't an option. Direct democracy, Roman-style republicanism, aristocracy, and monarchy all had serious flaws. None provided the structure and basic rights necessary for freedom, peace, and prosperity to thrive. So, the Founders created a new system by improving on the ideas of the ancient Hebrews, Greeks, Romans, and the more recent English. They gave us a constitutional republic. (See "Drafting and Ratification of the U.S. Constitution" in Session 7.)

Throughout the course, you will read about this new system and the principles the Founders decided were necessary for us to live in freedom, peace, and prosperity. These principles include *natural law and natural rights and consent of the governed.* In future sessions, you will read about other founding principles.

■ Key Terms

anarchy. Lack of government; a state of lawlessness or political disorder.

aristocracy. Rule by a small group of nobles who often inherit the right to rule. They are considered the experts.

bicameral. Having two branches or chambers, such as the House of Representatives and the Senate.

civil and **civic.** Relating to the state or its citizens.

consent of the governed. A phrase from the Declaration of Independence meaning that government gets its authority from the citizens, not from the ruler(s).

constitutional republic. A form of government, such as that of the United States, in which the executive and legislators are elected by the people to represent them and protect their private property rights and other rights of citizens. Elected officials must follow the rules of the nation's constitution, and their actions are subject to judicial review. (See the key term **republic** below.)

democracy. A form of government based on majority rule, in which voters elect their leaders and decisions are made when the majority wins by more than half the total votes.

federal. Relating to a system with one central government and divisions such as states, each with separate responsibilities and powers.

Founder. One of the leaders who founded the United States, especially one who attended the Constitutional Convention of 1787 and helped write the United States Constitution. (Also known as "Founding Father.")

inalienable, or **unalienable, rights.** Certain universal rights recognized by the Declaration of Independence and the U.S. Constitution that cannot be taken away or given away by government because they are naturally given to all individuals by their Creator at birth and are retained throughout life. (In law, a "lien" is a claim on the property of another.)

monarchy. A system of government ruled by a monarch (king, queen, emperor, or empress).

natural law, or **law of nature.** The unchanging God-given moral principles that form the basis for all human rights, behavior, and government.

natural rights. Rights under natural law that belong to every person.

Patriot. A person who supported the American colonies to end British oppression and gain freedom.

republic. A form of government in which citizens elect representatives to pass laws and a head of state (executive) to enforce them, and primary authority belongs to the citizens.

tyranny. Absolute power held by one person or a group that rules without respecting minority rights; oppressive power.

Discussion Questions

1. What did the Founders decide after studying various governments?

   They decided that no current or past system was ideal. Direct democracy, Roman-style republicanism, aristocracy, and monarchy did not provide the structure and basic rights necessary for freedom, peace, and prosperity to thrive. So, the Founders created a new system based on natural law and natural rights and consent of the governed and gave us a constitutional republic.

2. What aspects of the ancient Greek democracy did the Founders appreciate? What didn't they appreciate

   They appreciated the aspect of self-determinism, that individual citizens could vote and have a say in how the government was run, establishing laws that were to be universally applied. They did not appreciate that a simple majority vote could deny basic rights to those in the minority and that this could result in mob rule. This is why we have a constitutional republic that protects every citizen's natural rights—both from abuse of government power and from abuse by majority rule.

3. How was the ancient Roman Republic similar to the U.S. system of government? How was it different?

   Both accepted the principle of natural law: that our Creator created the universe and that natural law comes from God, not from the government. Both governments had two governing bodies, with the Assemblies in Rome similar to the U.S. House of Representatives in the United States, and both had a Senate. The major difference between the Roman Republic and the U.S. government is that U.S. Senators originally were elected by their respective states, whereas, in Rome, they inherited their position as members of the aristocracy. And in the end, the Roman Senate elected emperors, resulting in some of the worst tyrannies in history.

4. What principles did the Founders learn from Cicero in the Roman Republic before the republic devolved into tyranny?

   They accepted Cicero's belief in natural law coming from our Creator, not from government. This is key to the ideals of inalienable rights, consent of the governed, limited government, checks and balances, and a republican federal system.

5. Why was "consent of the governed" a revolutionary idea?

    Prior to the American Revolution, there had been very few examples of nations in which the general population of citizens had any direct power to govern themselves. Ancient Israel, Greece, and the Roman Republic all developed in ways that reflected "consent of the governed," as did English events leading up to the Glorious Revolution. The American Revolution was the most explicit example of this idea put into practice.

6. Why is the Magna Carta important?

    It was the first written constitution, in 1215, and protected the rights of the English, limited the power of the monarchy, and established the principle that everyone, including the monarch, was under the law.

7. Why was the English Parliament an advance in human rights?

    It advanced citizens' voices in the government and arose over time as a way to handle national issues. And it established the principle of no taxation without representation.

Lesson 2

The First Colonies:
Advancing Liberty in the New World

It [Plymouth settlement] opened a new chapter in the progress of events and in the history of colonizing countries. Hitherto, conquest, ambition, worldly glory, had often marked the settlement of newly discovered territory. . . . for the first time in the history of the world, the colonization of a new and great continent begins from the purest and profoundest religious convictions and principles.

Benjamin Franklin Morris, 1864

Compelling Question: How did the early American colonists develop the spirit of independence that eventually led them to break away from Great Britain and form a new independent nation?

Key Concepts

1. The North American British colonies were diverse. They were established to serve a wide variety of needs. What they all had in common was the shared heritage of English and Western European culture.

2. Roanoke and Virginia were founded primarily as economic ventures. Other colonies such as Plymouth and Massachusetts Bay were established primarily for religious reasons.

3. Both forms of colonies, whether motivated by financial gain or spiritual growth, demonstrated common trends of preferring self-governance and local control of their affairs.

Laying the Foundation

Human progress is rarely a straight line upward toward a goal. History is usually a mixture of failures and successes, setbacks and progress. The settling of our nation was no exception. In the colonies, rights were not granted to all people equally. Slavery was practiced in the colonies, and Native Americans lost lands and lives during colonization.

The colonists faced dire hardships in the early years. But their struggle for freedom led to profound benefits for all Americans today.

More than a century before the Declaration of Independence, English explorers and settlers sailed the stormy Atlantic Ocean to found the first permanent colonies in North America—Jamestown, Plymouth, and Massachusetts Bay. We'll learn about how these settlers laid the foundations for **free enterprise**, private property, representative government, **capitalism**, and religious freedom. These principles shaped the American character and culture. Notice these principles while reading our nation's founding documents.

Jamestown, Virginia: America's First Permanent English Colony

Sir Walter Raleigh sponsored an unsuccessful attempt in 1585 to colonize Roanoke Island offshore from present-day North Carolina. He planned to establish an English stronghold in North America to prevent Spain from claiming land north of Florida. But sadly—and mysteriously—this settlement, known as the "Lost Colony," vanished.

The plan to settle North America resumed in 1606 when King James I of England granted the Virginia Company of London a **charter** to found a colony and spread Christianity. The objective was also to discover gold, a water route to the Pacific Ocean, and the Lost Colony of Roanoke. This **joint stock company** financed the expedition and the colony by selling **shares of stock** to investors to raise **capital**. They believed that the colony would produce wealth and trade their products in England. The company, its investors, and the settlers all hoped to make a profit.

The settlers promised to work for the company in return for housing, food, supplies, and a share of stock in the company. The **shareholders** in England would be paid. After seven years, the company would grant the colonists 100 acres of land. At that time in England, the plan sounded beneficial to everyone. But was it successful?

The 40 sailors and 104 Englishmen and boys who survived the voyage sailed up the deep-water James River in May 1607. On a marshy peninsula, the settlers built a fort and established Jamestown, the first permanent English colony in North America.

Most of the colonists were of the gentry class (gentlemen who lived off rental payments and did no manual labor) and adventurers. Some craftsmen and laborers also came. But the colony had no women or families. The gentlemen and explorers expected to find gold and silver, as the Spanish had in Mexico and South America. The Jamestown men were disappointed that gold didn't wash up on the shores. The gentlemen didn't know how to farm. They thought that physical labor was beneath their status.

The settlers were unprepared for the harsh conditions in Virginia. They arrived during the area's most extreme drought in the past 770 years, according to recent scientific studies.

The drought led to contaminated drinking water, lack of food, and worsened relations with the native Powhatans. Neither the Powhatans nor the settlers could grow enough food. The corn crops on which they depended failed. The settlers couldn't leave the fort to hunt or fish for fear of being killed by the Powhatans. These conditions caused malnourishment and disease, including malaria. More than half the colonists died that disastrous first year.

The Virginia Company's actions made matters worse. King James appointed a president and council that ruled from London. Initially, the company owned all the land, buildings, and tools. Each person worked as he was able (or willing) for the company storehouse and the common good. Each person received food and other items he needed from this common store. The workers owned nothing other than personal items. As a result, no one had any incentive to work beyond the minimum necessary to receive his share from the common food supply. Creativity and risk-taking diminished because each colonist received an equal share of goods. Some of the men refused to work. And why should they?

When Captain John Smith became the Virginia Company's third president in September 1608, he refused to continue this practice. He knew that no society could flourish if it ignored a fundamental principle found in the Bible and familiar to settlers: if you don't work, you don't get to eat (except if sick or disabled). Under Smith's leadership, the colony flourished—more crops, new industries, and improved relations with the Native Americans. But this progress ended when Smith was injured and had to return to England in September 1609.

Then came the "Starving Time" of 1609–1610 at the height of the drought. The ship carrying more settlers and necessary supplies was stranded in Bermuda. The Powhatans, who also were starving, refused to provide food to the settlers. The shareholders demanded to be paid, but the company and colony were in financial ruin, and the settlers were just trying to survive. No one was profiting.

Sir Thomas Dale, the new acting governor, found the colony in disarray in 1611, so he took immediate and drastic action. To restore order and fix the failing colony, he imposed harsher discipline and **martial law**. In 1613, as governor, he also carried out company reforms. The most important reform was abandoning communal agriculture. He increased incentives by granting three acres of land to the early settlers and smaller plots to more recent arrivals. Crop planting and productivity increased because of private land ownership.

During this time, the extreme drought ended, and more settlers, including women, and supplies arrived. One of the newcomers, John Rolfe, married Chief Powhatan's daughter Pocahontas. Their marriage ushered in a period of improved relations between the tribe and the colonists. In 1614, Rolfe experimented with planting tobacco seeds from the Caribbean. His crop was so well received in England that it became Jamestown's first profitable export.

In 1618, Sir George Yeardley was appointed governor of the colony. The Virginia Company instructed him to carry out comprehensive reforms detailed in the new "Great Charter." Right away, Yeardley restored financial and political order and increased each settler's allotment of land to fifty acres. He also began transferring land from the Virginia Company to the settlers who occupied and worked it. Settlers received the land immediately that they had been promised after seven years of work for the company. Land and home ownership created a strong incentive to be productive because they benefitted personally from their own work. Conditions in the colony promptly improved.

Conditions further improved in 1619 when Sir Edwin Sandys, one of the Virginia Company's founders, was elected as the company's treasurer (a position similar to chairman). Although he never went to Virginia, he advocated free trade and increased immigration, including more women. He knew that families were essential for a stable society. He also encouraged more industries and exports. But tobacco still proved to be the most profitable crop, and it raised the colonists' standard of living.

Under Yeardley and Sandys, the General Assembly was formed and first met in 1619. It was the forerunner of two-house state legislatures and the U.S. Congress. The Virginia Company was represented in the General Assembly by the governor and an appointed council. Men who owned property elected 22 **burgesses** to the House of Burgesses.

Through representation in the House of Burgesses, these colonists gained the rights and privileges that landowners in England possessed.

In addition to the establishment of the House of Burgesses, in 1619 the first shipload of African slaves arrived in Virginia. The African slave trade had existed for centuries prior to the establishment of the British colonies in North America and had been a profitable business for Portuguese, Spanish, and Muslim traders operating throughout Africa.

Europeans and Muslims exploited native African tribal societies, trading goods for prisoners taken in intertribal conflict. The slave ship's original destination was Mexico, but after the fifty African slaves arrived in Jamestown, **chattel slavery** became one of several methods of meeting the labor demands of the new colony. But another generation passed before slavery took hold as crucial to Virginia's economy.

Few historical records exist regarding these African men, women, and children. They were likely put to work on the tobacco plantations surrounding Jamestown. Under English law, there was no hereditary slavery then. Some of the Africans became **indentured servants** rather than slaves. Indentured servanthood was a common means for English and other European settlers to pay for their travel to the colonies, where they sought better opportunities than were available to them in Europe.

While the Virginia Company never became profitable and was often mismanaged, the Jamestown Colony was a success by other measures. It established Great Britain's control of the territory and the spread of the English language, laws, religion, and culture to the New World. It showed that private property ownership gives people incentives, whereas **communalism** incentivizes laziness. And it laid the foundation for representative government in the future United States.

Plymouth Colony, Massachusetts: America's First Permanent New England Settlement

Like the Virginia Company of London, the Plymouth Company was founded as a joint stock company by the charter of 1606. Investors financed the settlers' trip, and the settlers were to repay them from profits made through shipping natural resources to England during the first seven years, after which the company would dissolve. During those years, the land would be held in common, and the laborers would work for a common goal. These contracts were the customary way of enabling people to settle in America who otherwise could not afford the voyage. But the Pilgrims disputed the company's communal policy from the beginning.

The settlers were mostly English Pilgrim families who had sought religious freedom in the Netherlands. They didn't think the Church of England could be reformed. They were called "separatists" because they separated from the Church of England to form independent local churches. After twelve years in the Netherlands, they wanted to live in a community of likeminded believers in America, where their children wouldn't be influenced by the Dutch culture and where they could prosper economically. The other part of the group was merchant adventurers. In 1620, they set out on the *Mayflower* for northern Virginia, but stormy weather veered the ship off course to Cape Cod, Massachusetts.

Before going ashore, the Pilgrim leaders drafted the **Mayflower Compact**. The compact was their governing document, which declared that their primary purpose was to form a government for "the Glory of God and advancement of the Christian faith." Along with the establishment of the Virginia House of Burgesses the year before in 1619, it laid the foundation for self-government and was a beginning step leading to the U.S. Constitution.

Although the colonists didn't have a charter to settle in Massachusetts, they decided to stay there rather than sail to Virginia. Supplies were dwindling and winter was setting in. Like the Jamestown settlers, the Pilgrims were unprepared for the harsh conditions—the cold winter, fierce storms, and "a hideous and desolate wilderness, full of wild beasts and wild men," in the words of their leader William Bradford.

They sailed on and finally found a suitable harbor for the *Mayflower* near an abandoned Indian site where they settled, naming it New Plymouth. As in Jamestown, about half the group died that terrible first winter from malnutrition, sickness, and exposure to the elements. Also, like Jamestown, Plymouth experienced a "Starving Time." Yet they persevered and built houses and gardens and crops in the spring of 1621.

The Pilgrim opposition to a communal economy and the breakdown of the system was evident in the settlement from the beginning. As more settlers arrived, some of whom paid their own way, the communal plan was abandoned in 1623. One-acre parcels were allotted to each person, including women and children, and productivity increased as it did in Jamestown.

The products shipped to England to pay off the debt to the investors were mainly furs, fish, and timber, but they didn't make a large profit. In 1627, Governor Bradford and eleven other men contracted to pay off the debt to the Plymouth Company, which was not accomplished until 1642. Finally, the Plymouth Colony merged with the more profitable Massachusetts Bay Colony in 1691.

Massachusetts Bay Colony: The Largest and Most Successful Settlement

The Massachusetts Bay Company was better organized and more business savvy than the Virginia Company. Formed in 1628 by capable Puritan businessmen, the company planned a profit-making endeavor as well as a colony where the settlers could practice their Christian beliefs. They obtained a charter from King Charles I to settle a broad area of New England. In 1629 while still in England, twelve Massachusetts Bay Company stockholders led by John Winthrop had the foresight to sign the Cambridge Agreement, which transferred the charter from England to Massachusetts. There it would become the colony's constitution. Unlike Jamestown and Plymouth, the Massachusetts Bay Colony would not be governed by stockholders in England. The company bought out stockholders who decided to stay in England. This provided for self-government in the colony and guaranteed their religious freedom.

The Massachusetts Bay Company was also better prepared for the journey and included a greater number of passengers than the Virginia and Plymouth Companies' voyages. In 1630, more than 700 colonists on eleven ships established a permanent settlement on the site they named New Boston. Soon the population increased to about 1,000. The settlers were mainly prominent, well-educated citizens of England and their families. Some were former members of Parliament.

Yet they too suffered hardships in the early years. Their crude dwellings provided little protection against the long, harsh New England winters. An estimated 200 colonists died the first year from lack of food, disease, and the elements. The supplies from England they depended on dwindled. They couldn't always obtain fresh water. And the New England land was not suitable for largescale agriculture. Like the colonists in Jamestown and Plymouth, they had to be on guard against Indian attacks.

But by 1640, the population of the colony had soared to more than 20,000 settlers. Entire congregations fled persecution from the King of England in what became known as the Great Puritan Migration. The quick population expansion, compared to the other colonies, contributed to their success. Soon they moved to areas surrounding Boston where they founded many farming towns and villages and eventually established the new colonies of Connecticut and Rhode Island.

Communalism was practiced to some extent along with private property ownership. The colonists planted communal gardens and farms. Property ownership didn't give them the right to vote, as it did in Jamestown. Unlike the settlers in Jamestown, they grew a variety of crops. If one crop failed, they had others to feed their families and to sell. In the early years, the colonists depended on imports from England. Investments by wealthy immigrants and trade with other colonies, the West Indies, England, and European nations boosted the colony's economy. By 1632, their merchant fleet numbered about 200 ships, which transported fish, fur, and lumber in trade for needed supplies.

Despite the hardships they faced, the Puritans persisted in improving living conditions and building a successful colony. One factor initially was their widely agreed upon religious beliefs. Their shared faith sustained them. They believed that God was in control of whatever happened, so they viewed hardships as lessons from God. They also had a strong "Puritan work ethic," meaning that personal virtue was to be found in hard work and self-sacrifice. The Puritans believed in individual responsibility and self-discipline. And they believed that they were God's chosen people who had a mission. Winthrop wrote, "For we must consider that we shall be as a city upon on a hill. The eyes of all people are upon us."

The towns they founded each had a church, called a "meeting house," with its own governing body. All the men who were church members met in town-hall meetings to govern the town. Puritan government initially was a **theocracy** based on biblical law. The Puritans viewed their charter as a **covenant** between God and the colony to build a city that would honor God's commandments. Because they believed so strongly in biblical law, they did not practice tolerance toward those who held different beliefs. Only **freemen**, who were required to be church members, could vote in town-hall meetings.

The General Court, consisting of all freemen, elected officers and made laws for the colony. Winthrop was elected the first governor in 1630. Later the General Court was divided into two separate bodies: the General Court and the Council of Assistants, which handled court cases. Before a law could be passed, both bodies had to agree on it.

The colonists began demanding that the power of the government be curbed. They wanted the laws of the colony to be written as a constitutional protection of their personal freedoms. The resulting document, the Massachusetts Body of Liberties, was presented to the town governments for their feedback, and the General Council finally adopted it in 1641, after years of opposition. The document cited the Magna Carta. (See Session 1.) Most of the Liberties dealt with individuals' rights in court cases. Among these rights were assurance of **bail**, a speedy trial, equal protection under the law, no **double jeopardy**, and no cruel punishment. The rights of women, children, and servants were protected. Many of these liberties appear in the U.S. Constitution.

During this time, slavery was practiced throughout all human societies. It was first legalized in North America by a provision in the Massachusetts Body of Liberties. However, slavery was not widely practiced in the Massachusetts Bay Colony, except for household labor for wealthy colonists.

The Puritans had a high regard for learning. The intellectual life in the colony was on a level not seen in the other colonies. The Puritans believed that children should be educated so that they could read the Bible and ancient Greek and Roman classic literature. Towns provided publicly funded education for children. Harvard College (now Harvard University) was founded in 1636 to educate ministers.

The Massachusetts Bay Colony grew and prospered as the **commonwealth** of Massachusetts Bay. Increasingly, Kings Charles I and his successor Charles II exercised more authority over the colonies and demanded taxes from them as British subjects. Besides restricting free speech, they clamped down on the colony's independence and freedom, which caused tensions to rise. The colonists continued to trade with countries other than England, in violation of the Navigation Acts. They ran an illegal mint to make their own coins. And the colony's General Court passed religious laws that conflicted with laws of England. For these actions, the king suspended the colony's charter and ended the commonwealth in 1684.

As the generations passed, the Massachusetts Bay colonists did not forget how Great Britain had trampled on the freedoms of their ancestors in the late 1600s. It is no surprise that the colony became the birthplace of the American Revolution, led by Samuel and John Adams, John Hancock, Paul Revere, and others. And the first shots in the war were fired at the Battles of Lexington and Concord in Massachusetts.

■ Key Terms

bail. An amount of money a person accused of a crime pays to a court of law so that he or she can be released from custody until the trial. The payment is a way of making certain that the person will return to court for the trial.

Burgess. A member of the Virginia House of Burgesses, the first elected legislature of a British colony. Each of the eleven colonial settlements were entitled to two burgesses. The House of Burgesses was part of the General Assembly, whose other members were appointed.

charter. A written grant by a governing body's legislature or ruling authority by which a company, college, or city is founded and its rights are defined.

chattel slavery. The ownership of human beings as property that can be bought, sold, given, and inherited, thereby denying them their natural rights.

commonwealth. A nation, state, or other political unit, such as one founded on law and united by compact or agreement of the people for the common good; one in which supreme authority is vested in the people.

communalism. The collective ownership and use of property.

compact. A voluntary agreement, or contract, between two or more parties, for example the Mayflower Compact. (Also known as "**covenant**.")

double jeopardy. The trying of a person twice for the same offense.

free enterprise. An economic system in which businesses compete for profit without much government control. Products, prices, and services are determined by the market, not the government.

freeman. A man who has full rights of citizenship, including the right to vote.

indentured servant. A person who signs a voluntary or forced contract to work for another for a specified time, especially in return for payment of travel expenses and maintenance.

joint stock company. A forerunner of the modern corporation that was organized for enterprises requiring large amounts of capital. Money was raised by selling shares to investors, who became partners in the undertaking.

martial law. Military government, involving the suspension of ordinary law.

shareholder. Someone who owns a share of property or stock in a company.

stock. The capital raised by a company through the issue of shares.

theocracy. A system of government based on religious law.

Discussion Questions

1. Compare the Jamestown, Plymouth, and Massachusetts Bay Colonies. How were they similar? How were they different?

   They were similar in that they were settled by colonists who shared a common religious heritage from England (although the Plymouth and Massachusetts colonies were explicit religious communities). They were financed by investors in England who purchased stock in new companies established just for each mission. And they all nearly failed early on because they were ill-prepared for the harsh weather, and many were simply ill-equipped for frontier life.

   The three colonies were founded at different times. It became successively easier to establish a colony as knowledge about the American continent grew. And it became easier to establish colonies with larger numbers and more supplies. For example, 144 arrived to establish the Jamestown Colony in 1607; 700 established the Massachusetts Bay Colony 23 years later in 1630.

   Another difference was the demographics of colonists who first arrived. Jamestown settlers were mainly gentlemen and adventurers, who had no farming skills. The Plymouth settlers included families. The Massachusetts Bay colonists were the wealthiest and best educated. Entire congregations settled there.

2. What factors led to hardships and failures?

   Harsher winters and hotter summers than in Great Britain made life in America hard, especially for those who came without experience in farming, hunting and self-protection against hostile natives. Initially, they built crude dwellings from scratch that did not protect well against the elements. One of the problems in Jamestown was that many of the new colonists, were unwilling to work for a variety of reasons, including their perceived place in society as "gentlemen." The practice of gathering all food supplies into a common storehouse made the situation worse.

3. What factors led to successes?

   Instituting private property ownership, a practice rooted in English law, helped motivate the colonists to produce more goods. The settlers learned survival skills, such as building, farming, and fishing and hunting techniques, and they produced goods to trade and sell. In the Massachusetts colonies, diversification of crops and the strong Puritan work ethic also contributed to their success. In Virginia, the success of the tobacco crops increased their wealth.

4. How did each colony advance liberty?

   Jamestown was the first successful permanent English colony in America. Despite its early difficulties, by the middle of the 1600s, it offered opportunities for land and freedom to those in Great Britain and Europe willing to accept the risk. The first bicameral legislature—the House of Burgesses—was established in Jamestown. Through representation in the House of Burgesses, these colonists gained the rights and privileges that landowners in England possessed. The Plymouth Colony is known for the Mayflower Compact. It laid the foundation for self-government and was a beginning step leading to the U.S. Constitution.

   The colonists of the Massachusetts Bay Colony began demanding that the power of the government be curbed. They wanted the laws of the colony to be written as a constitutional protection of their personal freedoms. The General Court and the Council of Assistants loosely set the stage for creation of two bodies to determine the law—a forerunner of the U.S. Senate and House of Representatives. Included in the "Massachusetts Body of Liberties" were assurances of bail, a speedy trial, equal protection under the law, no double jeopardy, and no cruel punishment. The rights of women, children, and servants were protected. Many of these liberties appear in the U.S. Constitution.

5. What colonial events contributed to the colonies rebelling against Great Britain?

   For more than a century, the colonists increasingly developed self-reliance and independence from Great Britain. The colonists established their own governing bodies, eventually produced their own coins, and went against England by trading with countries other than England. Increasingly, King Charles I and his successor Charles II tightened their grip on the colonies, asserting their authority in opposition to colonists' rights.

Map of the Thirteen Colonies (First States)

Lesson 3

The Enlightenment and Foundations of American Government

[W]ithout virtue there can be no liberty.
Dr. Benjamin Rush, 1787

Compelling Question: How did the principles of the Enlightenment influence the Founders in writing the documents that form the foundation of the United States of America?

Key Concepts

1. The Age of Enlightenment, 1687–1789, was a period of significant intellectual advancement across Europe, and particularly in Great Britain (England and Scotland).

2. The Enlightenment emphasized logic, rational argument, and scientific thinking.

3. The rights of Englishmen enjoyed by colonists had their roots in the history of England, especially the Glorious Revolution of 1688.

4. Traditional English private property rights were strengthened in colonial America by the influence of Enlightenment philosophers who argued that such rights were natural rights.

American Government—The Great Experiment

America's form of government was unlike any other form of government since it recognized Americans' inalienable **natural rights**. Even today most other governments grant only civil rights to their citizens. As John Quincy Adams expressed in 1837:

> The revolution had been exclusively popular and democratic, and the Declaration had announced that the only object of the institution of governments among men was to secure their unalienable rights, and that they derived their just powers from the consent of the governed.

John Quincy Adams (our sixth President, serving from 1825 to 1829) was uniquely qualified to comment on the distinctive character of the American government. His father, John Adams (our second President), was one of the most important Patriots serving at the Second Continental Congress, and John Quincy witnessed the birth of the United States during the Revolution.

As discussed in Session 1, the origins of American government come from the history and heritage of Western civilization. The founding of the United States was influenced by Judeo- Christian culture, the history of Ancient Greece and Rome, and the history and liberties of England. (See Session 1.)

The Founders drew not only on their classical studies and excellent educations, but also on new documents and philosophical writings that were available to them, including those of Sir William Blackstone. The beginning of the Enlightenment is generally recognized to have occurred in 1687 with the publication of Sir Isaac Newton's great mathematical text *Principia*. The **Enlightenment** was focused on the use of logic and reason as the best way to understand the world and how it worked. Empirical knowledge, meaning "scientific," or that which can be measured, calculated, and tested by experimentation, was believed to be more reliable and valid than other ways of knowing. Enlightenment writers and publications influenced the Founders in many ways. Fortunately, the Founders were Christians, deists, or Jewish, and they were not swayed by the radical *philosophes* (French for "philosophers") in France who were opposed to religion and intolerant. Following are some of the most significant examples of Enlightenment documents that were influential with the Founders.

English Bill of Rights (1689). In 1688, King James II, the unpopular Roman Catholic king of England, attempted to seize total power and be recognized as an absolute ruler, subject to no limits. Parliament, having previously fought to ensure that this didn't happen, moved to depose James from the throne. They invited James's daughter Mary and her husband William, who were Protestant, to become queen and king of England. Thus, England changed from a Catholic to a Protestant nation. Monarchs never again could be Catholic.

This change is now known as "The Glorious Revolution." After establishing William III and Mary II as king and queen, Parliament passed a set of laws placing strict limits on the new monarchs. Included in these limits was a list of individual rights the Crown (king or queen) was required to honor.

- Without the permission of Parliament, the Crown could not tax the people.
- Citizens had the right to petition the king (or queen) and would not be punished for merely asking for consideration.
- Raising or keeping an army within the kingdom in time of peace, unless Parliament

- approved, was against the law.
- Citizens were assured that they would not be subject to cruel and unusual punishments.
- Election of members of Parliament would be protected from abuse and be free of coercion from the Crown.
- Freedom of speech and debates in Parliament would be protected.

The English Bill of Rights advanced Enlightenment principles by removing the Crown's religious authority to rule by the divine right of kings. Instead, monarchs became subject to Parliament, just as citizens were. The Founders assumed that they were protected by the English Bill of Rights, just as any other British subject living in Great Britain could expect. The violations of the English Bill of Rights ultimately led the Founders to take the bold step of revolution against King George III in the Revolutionary War. Further, the English Bill of Rights influenced and shaped the first ten amendments of the U.S. Constitution, known as the "Bill of Rights." (See Sessions 13, 14, and 15.)

John Locke's *Two Treatises of Government* (1689). Published in England the same year as the English Bill of Rights, John Locke's work carefully considers the question of whether or not people have a natural right to freedom. Locke concludes that such a right does exist. The right to freedom is a natural law that no man-made government is justified in taking away. Locke's *First Treatise* addresses how the idea of natural rights and natural laws respecting individual freedoms are consistent with the Judeo-Christian ethical and moral codes. (See Session 1.) His *Second Treatise* delves into how those natural rights are expressed. Two well-known passages follow:

> Man being born, as has been proved, with a title to perfect freedom . . . has by nature a power . . . ***to preserve his property, that is, his life, liberty and estate, against the injuries and attempts by other men***. (Chapter VII, Section 87, emphasis added)

> But if they have set limits to the duration of their legislature, and made this supreme power in any person, or assembly, only temporary; or else, when by the miscarriages of this in authority, it is forfeited; upon the forfeiture, or at the determination of the time set, it reverts to the society, and ***the people have a right to act supreme, and continue the legislative in themselves; or erect a new form, or under the old form place it in new hands, as they think good.*** (Chapter XIX, Section 243, emphasis added)

Notice how in these passages Locke, a philosopher, is making the case that people have a natural right to have and protect their own lives, their individual freedom, and their own property.

Likewise, Locke argues that it is the people living together as a community who have the power to organize and implement a government for themselves. The legitimacy of a government is constituted by the authority of its people.

Baron Charles de Montesquieu's *De l'esprit des lois (The Spirit of Laws, 1748)*. This work illustrates that the Enlightenment spirit was by no means confined to Great Britain. Montesquieu, a French philosopher and political writer, who was also a Christian, attempted to conduct a scientific comparison of the world's different systems of government. Montesquieu was an accomplished and widely read scholar. His work was well-known to the Founders. A sample of his writing follows:

> In every government there are three sorts of power; the legislative; the executive, in respect to things dependent on the law of nations; and the executive, in regard to things that depend on the civil law.

By virtue of the first, the prince or magistrate enacts temporary or perpetual laws, and amends or abrogates [nullifies or abolishes] those that have been already enacted. By the second, he makes peace or war, sends or receives embassies; establishes the public security, and provides against invasions. By the third, he punishes criminals, or determines the disputes that arise between individuals. The latter we shall call the judiciary power, and the other simply the executive power of the state.

The political liberty of the subject is a tranquility of mind, arising from the opinion each person has of his safety. In order to have this liberty, it is requisite the government be so constituted as one man need not be afraid of another.

When the legislative and executive powers are united in the same person, or in the same body of magistrates, there can be no liberty; because apprehensions may arise, lest the same monarch or senate should enact tyrannical laws, to execute them in a tyrannical manner.

Again, there is no liberty if the power of judging be not separated from the legislative and executive powers. Were it joined with the legislative, the life and liberty of the subject would be exposed to arbitrary control, for the judge would then be the legislator. Were it joined to the executive power, the judge might behave with all the violence of an oppressor.

There would be an end of everything were the same man, or the same body, whether of the nobles or of the people to exercise those three powers that of enacting laws, that of executing the public resolutions, and that of judging the crimes or differences of individuals.

These passages by Locke and Montesquieu all point to specific aspects and attributes later found in the Declaration of Independence and eventually the U.S. Constitution. They illustrate that the Founders were working from well-established principles within English law and tradition that included respect for individual rights, respect for private property, the rule of law, and the principle of separation of powers of government.

America's Wealth—An Enlightenment Explanation

Adam Smith's *An Inquiry into the Nature and Causes of the Wealth of Nations* (1776). Smith was a Scottish Enlightenment philosopher and economist in the mid-to-late 1700s. His work, *The Wealth of Nations,* is considered one of the most influential documents ever written. Published the same year as the Declaration of Independence, the economic principles detailed in this book were well-known to the Founders. These principles included private property rights and helped to determine the role the government would play in promoting the growth of the national economy in the newly independent United States.

Smith understood that people can make better informed decisions about their own welfare than can any bureaucrat or ruler, no matter how well schooled or benevolent. And he was the first to understand and reveal that a marketplace where everyone makes his or her own decisions will naturally tend toward the best fit between the goods that are available for sale (supply), and the price that buyers are most willing to pay (demand).

Self-reliance was the hallmark of those who colonized the New World, fought the Revolutionary War, and founded our nation. Without being self-reliant, they could not have prospered as they did under the conditions of hardship, danger, and geographic isolation they had to overcome to create this free, rich, and powerful nation. And being self-reliant, the colonists were used to making their own decisions about what to produce and how to trade with each other. After more than 150 years of colonial experience following the settlement of Jamestown, the Founders understood the benefits of free markets in which people make their own decisions and benefit from what they produce.

Smith referred to property created or bought for the purpose of producing goods or services as "capital." He was among the first to recognize that a nation's wealth is determined by what it can produce, and what it can produce is determined by the capital its people have accumulated. **Capitalism** is the economic system in which individuals have the freedom to invest their capital (their property) in businesses, ventures, or opportunities that will make a profit for them. Such an investment might be in buying and selling merchandise or building a factory or purchasing a larger piece of land to plant crops. An individual with a small amount of capital might choose to save it in a bank (low risk) and earn interest on the savings (low return). An individual with a larger amount of capital might choose to invest in a new business (higher risk) that offers the chance for high profits (higher return). Capitalism is based on the principle that people tend to make the best decisions for their own benefit and the good of their community if given the freedom to control their own property. And because more goods and services are produced under free market capitalism (than in a state-owned **collectivist** system), there is more profit available to tax, which provides more revenue to pay for services for those who cannot provide for themselves.

The Founders recognized that the potential for growth and prosperity for the United States depended on the proper respect for the natural rights of its citizens. The new freedom enjoyed by the colonists (compared to the oppression they experienced in Europe) allowed the development of a uniquely American identity. And the best ideas of the Enlightenment—focusing on rational thought and science— complemented their Judeo-Christian roots. Their brilliant understanding of history, including about ancient Greece, the Roman Republic, and the rights of Englishmen, made for a solid foundation to create the Organic Laws of the United States of America.

The Necessity for Virtue

The Founders also recognized that the same character traits common to the American people, which had promoted the growth of the colonies in the century and a half before independence, must be tempered with **virtue**. The colonists were willing to work hard, they lived within their means, they respected the rights and property of others, and they were independent. Although there was no national or state religion for the new country, the Founders had a deep and abiding respect for Judeo-Christian ethics and morals.

Furthermore, many of those who would be setting the foundations and raising the walls of the new nation believed strongly in the Enlightenment idea that it was more important that the people be consistent in a form of religion, not that it must be any one specific creed, sect, or denomination. The success of America would be dependent upon the extent to which its citizens could govern themselves, rather than succumbing to the temptation of expecting the government to be responsible for controlling and caring for them. Virtue, both practiced by individuals and as an expression of civic duty, was understood to be an inseparable element necessary for America to progress. Without the foundation of a virtuous people, governments would have to continually pass more laws to cover new injustices. As John Adams said in 1798, "Our constitution was made only for a moral and religious people. It is wholly inadequate to the government of any other."

Correcting Injustices and Expanding Civil Rights for all Americans

Slavery is wrong—yet it has existed all over the world for more than 5,000 years. It was commonplace throughout the world at the time of the colonies in America. (It still exists in many parts of the world. Today, 167 countries still have slavery, affecting about 46 million people. Modern slavery is also known as "human trafficking.")

The founders knew it was essential to unite all thirteen colonies to fight for and maintain independence from Great Britain, and they were forced to compromise over the slavery issue. However, the national consensus in the late 1700s was that Congress should prevent the expansion of slavery. Most Founders believed the next generation would abolish it and that it was prudent to take gradual steps toward prohibiting it. For example, they did not allow the spread of slavery into the Northwest Territory (Section XIV, Article 6 of the Northwest Ordinance of 1787).

Sadly, more than 600,000 men and women lost their lives in the Civil War, which was fought primarily over slavery. This led to the elimination of slavery and Amendment XIII, which was ratified in 1865. (Read "The Compromise on Slavery" and "Changing American Culture Regarding Slavery and Voting Rights" in Session 7.)

The culture of freedom and recognition that all Americans must be treated equally under the law eventually resulted in many laws to correct abuse of African Americans and Native American Indians. The fact that it took hundreds of years to replace inhumane treatment speaks volumes about the basic nature of human beings. From the colonial era through westward expansion, many Native American Indians lost their lives in wars against the settlers and succumbed to diseases from Europe to which they lacked immunity. But Native American tribes also fought to the death against each other and treated captured members of other tribes as slaves. And they killed thousands of white settlers. (Read "Founders Attempts to Abolish Slavery and Abuse of Indians" in Session 6.)

From the colonial era until today, Americans of all races have experienced positive interactions with each other—but sometimes interactions have been abusive and unjust. This is common among all peoples of the world, from the beginning of time. (See Session 17: "Balancing War-Time Threats and Civil Rights.") But American history includes stories of thousands of African Americans, Native American Indians, and men and women of all races, fighting alongside white Europeans as compatriots in the American War of Independence. Additionally, they fought together in the Civil War, World War I, World War II, and in every other war since.

■ Key Terms

capitalism. An economic and political system based on private property rights and in which a country's trade and industry are controlled by private owners rather than by the government.

collectivist. Relating to a political group or economic system in which a group controls the production and distribution of goods and property is owned by the group rather than privately. Also, it can describe a person who holds such views.

divine right of kings. The principle or belief that kings (or queens) derive their authority from God, not from the people they rule.

Enlightenment. The European intellectual movement (1687–1789) that emphasized rational, empirical, and scientific thinking and often rejected traditional religious, social, and political ideas.

natural law, or **law of nature.** The unchanging God-given moral principles that form the basis for all human rights, behavior, and government.

natural rights. Rights under natural law that belong to every person.

virtue. Behavior showing high moral standards.

 Discussion Questions

1. In what ways did the English Bill of Rights limit the authority of the Crown (the king or queen)?

   The English Bill of Rights signaled the end of divine rights of kings, ended rule by the monarchy, and established a parliamentary, or republican, system of government. It made it illegal for the Crown to levy money (tax or raise revenues or take money from the treasury) without the permission of Parliament. It made it illegal for the Crown to punish anyone who petitioned the Crown for consideration. The king could not keep military forces in readiness on a full-time basis without Parliament's authorization. Subjects (as long as they were Protestant) were allowed to have arms, implying a militia existed separate from the army. The Crown could not interfere with Parliamentary elections or proceedings.

2. How did John Locke define *property* in his *Second Treatise*?

   The three elements defining a man's property are his life, his liberty, and his estate (the possessions he owns and might pass on to his children). Notice how these are similar to the Declaration of Independence's "life, liberty, and the pursuit of happiness."

3. Why are property rights important?

   Ownership of private property is key to self-determination and freedom. If citizens cannot own their own property, they cannot keep the fruits of their own labor, and they lose initiative to work to benefit themselves and their own families. Society devolves and productivity declines when everything is owned by the state or held in a common storehouse.

4. According to Locke, when do the people have the authority to dissolve and reform their government?

   The government might be dissolved whenever its term of service is completed or it abuses its authority or whenever the people, "(who) have a right to act supreme," choose to do so.

5. Montesquieu describes a government as having three sorts of power. What are the three he describes?

   He describes government as having legislative power (to write or amend laws), an executive power for attending to national security and diplomacy, and an executive power for attending to domestic peace (judiciary).

LESSON THREE | 25

6. What circumstances does Montesquieu say will lead to a loss of liberty?

   He says that political liberty is maintained as long as the three separate powers (legislative, executive, and judicial) are kept divided, so that no one man or body of government could control two or more of them together. This is an illustration of the principle of separation of powers seen in the U.S. Constitution.

7. Why did the Founders believe that virtue was necessary for self-government?

   Most of Founders were religious, and they knew that without a virtuous people upholding the law and electing virtuous people, the laws would not be sufficient to keep the peace and treat people justly. They knew that as virtue declines, more and more laws would be needed to deal with those who want to escape the spirit of the law.

Lesson 4

Declaration of Independence and the Causes of Revolution

Give me liberty or give me death!
Patrick Henry, Address to the Second Virginia Convention, March 23, 1775

Compelling Question: How does the Declaration of Independence reflect the events leading to the American Revolution and the Founders' concepts of freedom?

Key Concepts

1. The colonists were not protesting the amount of taxation but rather the process of taxation. Hence the motto, "No taxation without representation."

2. King George III and Parliament violated the natural rights and the English liberties of American colonists. Therefore, the Declaration lists 27 abuses committed against the colonists as justification for independence.

3. George Washington led the Continental Army to victory and achieved significance as a symbol of the American republic based on natural law principles.

4. The French alliance greatly helped Americans with arms, men, and moneys. The French Navy played a crucial role in blockading British General Charles Cornwallis at Yorktown.

Causes of the American Revolution and Indictment of George III and Parliament

The causes of the American Revolution were the abuses by King George III and the acts of legislation from Parliament. The colonists believed that the British government had acted arbitrarily in violating the right of the colonists to rule themselves. The Declaration lists these abuses in the form of a legal **indictment** directed against the king. Because of these abuses, the colonists declared that the king and Parliament no longer had any authority over the colonies.

French and Indian War

As France expanded into the Ohio River Valley from 1754 to 1763, it fought with Britain for control of North America. Both sides forged alliances with Indians to help fight their battles. The French and Indian War (known as the "Seven Years' War in Europe"), set the stage for the American Revolution. Great Britain and her allies successfully defeated France, removing a military threat from the American colonies. The colonists expected to settle the newly acquired lands. King George III had a responsibility to protect all of his North American subjects, both colonists and Native American Indians. The Royal Proclamation of 1763 established a boundary line separating the colonies from the lands provided for the Native Americans and forbade colonial settlements west of the line. This ignored the reality of an ever-growing population on the frontier and the colonists' desire to expand westward.

Bringing the North American Colonies under British Control

King George III's Parliament instituted increasingly hostile actions against the colonies. British soldiers held many colonists' religious beliefs in contempt. Colonial leaders were threatened for holding meetings of any sort. The British government saw the colonists as the beneficiaries of the new land won in the French and Indian War. Therefore, the government thought the colonies should help pay the debts Parliament incurred on their behalf. So, Parliament imposed a series of new taxes and more strictly enforced collection of existing taxes on the colonists.

Parliament passed the Stamp Act in 1765, which required a stamp on newspapers, documents, and legal papers. The Townshend Acts, passed in 1767, taxed glass, lead, tea, and paper. Americans protested by boycotting British goods. The duties, except the tax on tea, were repealed, but Parliament insisted it still had the authority to tax the colonists.

In most ways, the colonists had governed and taxed themselves for decades. The moves by Parliament to impose and enforce taxes violated rights guaranteed to the colonists, as Englishmen, in their colonial charters. Parliament was violating the rights of colonists, who had no elected representatives in Parliament. This meant they had no voice, yet they were still expected to pay taxes. "No taxation without representation" became the rallying cry of the colonists.

The **East India Company** controlled the British tea trade. Americans' **boycott** of English goods hurt the company's profits. Parliament passed the Tea Act giving the East India Company a monopoly. The colonists protested the Act because it hurt merchants, and it set the precedent for Parliament granting a **monopoly** in the colonies. In protest, **Sons of Liberty** disguised themselves as American Indians and dumped chests of tea in Boston Harbor on December 13, 1773. At the time, only the vessel carrying the despised tea was boarded, and only the tea was damaged. No one was injured, and the ship itself was unharmed. Today we call this the "Boston Tea Party."

Parliament responded to the Boston Tea Party by passing what the Americans called the **"Intolerable Acts"** (1774). These acts

- closed the Port of Boston;
- replaced the government of Massachusetts with a military governor;
- allowed British officials accused of crimes in Massachusetts to return to England for trial;
- required Americans to be deported to England; and
- forced the citizens of Boston to allow soldiers to live in people's private homes.

The First Continental Congress met in response to these acts of aggression and domination under the Intolerable Acts. The Virginia House of Burgesses met to condemn what was being done to Massachusetts. The Royal Governor responded by disbanding the Burgesses, which had represented the people of Virginia for nearly 150 years. Thus, in March 1775, Patrick Henry uttered his immortal words, "Give me liberty, or give me death!"

Three weeks later, the British sent troops to Concord to seize colonial supplies of weapons and powder. On the Lexington village green, colonial militia met the British Army, and a shot was fired, known famously as "the shot heard round the world." The British were forced to retreat and suffered many casualties. The Battles of Lexington and Concord were the first battles of the Revolutionary War (1775–1783). The British fought their way back to Boston, opposed by **Minutemen** and local **militias**. One hundred twenty-two colonists died at Lexington and Concord. The Battle of Bunker Hill followed, which the British won but with heavy losses. The British then returned to Boston for the Siege of Boston.

"When in the Course of Human Events"

The Siege of Boston lasted from April 19, 1775, until March 17, 1776. During that time, colonial leaders, meeting at the Second Continental Congress in Philadelphia, authorized the formation of the Continental Army to resist the British. George Washington, a colonel of the Virginia Militia, was commissioned by the Congress to be Commanding General of the new American Army. Under his leadership, the Americans won the Siege of Boston.

However, the British Army—the best trained, best equipped, and most successful military force of its day—was preparing to resume the fight by attacking General Washington and the Continental Army in New York during the summer of 1776. At the same time, the Second Continental Congress was preparing the document that would formally sever the thirteen British colonies from the Crown. The Declaration of Independence had to present the argument that the American colonies were acting righteously in rejecting British authority and that their case for revolution was just and honorable.

The opening paragraphs of the Declaration of Independence summarize the political beliefs held by the Founders. Recall from Session 3 that these men were influenced strongly by recent Enlightenment thinkers (Montesquieu, Locke), the expansion of individual rights resulting from the late English Civil Wars, and the centuries-old traditions of personal rights enjoyed by Englishmen.

These deeply held concepts of freedom are brought into sharp focus and set the stage for all that follows.

"A Long Train of Abuses"

Following the soaring concepts of freedom expressed in the first two paragraphs, the Declaration then makes the colonies' case against the king. It lays the responsibility for the British government's heavy-handed abuses of power squarely at King George III's feet. The Declaration of Independence is framed to make the case before the eyes of the world that the revolution then underway was just, righteous, and most importantly, legal.

What follows are 27 separate accusations, leveled at King George III personally. Each one begins with the phrase, "He has . . ." or lists actions he has authorized, actions that violate traditional rights of Englishmen. These accusations might be thought of as the opening statement by the prosecutor at a criminal trial, laying out the case against the accused. And not surprisingly, the three paragraphs following the "Long Train of Abuses" seek to make the case that the colonies had made every reasonable effort to avoid conflict and seek reconciliation with the Crown. As their efforts had been rebuffed and rejected, the Founders had no choice but to seek independence.

Conclusion of the Declaration

The Declaration of Independence concludes with an appeal to God, declares the independence of the colonies from Great Britain, and that as independent states, they become sovereign states. The full powers of government include declaring war and peace, forming treaties with foreign nations, and all the inherent powers related to sovereignty. Finally, the signers relied upon the providence of God to guide the affairs of men and pledged their lives, possessions, and honor—everything they valued—to the cause of liberty.

The five authors of the Declaration of Independence were Thomas Jefferson of Virginia, Roger Sherman of Connecticut, Benjamin Franklin of Pennsylvania, Robert R. Livingston of New York, and John Adams of Massachusetts. The primary author was Thomas Jefferson.

Brief History of the American Revolutionary War

The American Revolutionary War had four phases.

Phase 1 lasted from 1775 into mid-1776. The colonists seized the positions of government from the Royalists (loyal to King George III). The colonists were successful after the Battles of Lexington and Concord. The British had to fight their way back to Boston, suffering great losses. The Battle of Bunker Hill and the Siege of Boston followed. During the 11-month Siege of Boston, General George Washington began to form an army and forced the British to evacuate Boston.

During phase 2, from July 1776 until 1777, the British were on the offense. They captured New York in August 1776 and nearly destroyed the Continental Army by trapping them on Long Island and Manhattan. Washington retreated across New York and into New Jersey in October 1776. American fortunes appeared to be failing. But a turning point came with some stirring victories. Washington crossed the Delaware River to defeat the enemy at Trenton and Princeton in late 1776 and early 1777. General Horatio Gates defeated a British invasion from Canada into New York, which attempted to divide the colonies at the Battles of Saratoga, September–October 1777. This victory was the first major defeat of the British Army by the Continental Army since 1775, and it led to recognition of the United States by the king of France.

The third phase opened in 1778 when France allied with the states. The French supplied arms and men to America while forcing the British to defend their empire. The British engaged in a southern campaign, capturing Savannah (Georgia) in December 1778. In May 1780, the British seized Charleston (South Carolina) and won the Battle of Camden (New Jersey) in August 1780. American forces engaged in guerilla warfare that featured hit-and-run attacks, which inflicted greater damage on the British while preventing great losses for the Americans. The American General Nathanael Greene, who replaced General Gates after the Battle of Camden, encouraged this method of fighting. The Americans fought major battles at Kings Mountain (October 1780), Cowpens (January 1781), Guilford Courthouse (March 1781), and Eutaw Springs (September 1781), which depleted the British Army in the South. These victories allowed Washington to defeat General Cornwallis by trapping him in a siege at Yorktown (Virginia, October 1781) while the French Navy prevented the British from resupplying and evacuating by sea. British military operations virtually ended with the Battle of Yorktown.

With the decisive defeat of Cornwallis at Yorktown, the Revolutionary War entered the fourth, and final, phase. No more major battles occurred. In spite of poorly paid soldiers and threats of mutiny, General Washington managed to keep the Continental Army functioning until the very end of the war. The Treaty of Paris was signed in April 1783, ending the long eight-year struggle for independence.

Washington peacefully turned over his military commission and returned to his home of Mount Vernon, Virginia. He was revered so highly that some called for him to be made king, which he rejected. His actions set the foundation for civilian control and authority over the military and affirmed the traditional role of the citizen-soldier in America. And ever since, as our first president, George Washington has been known as "the father of our country."

■ Key Terms

boycott. An organized refusal to buy certain products. A boycott seeks to exert economic pressure on a government or business in order to force a change in laws or policies.

East India Company. The British trading company that dominated trade with India.

French and Indian War. The war from 1754 to 1763 (fought mainly in the upper Ohio Valley and Great Lakes region), in which the British defeated the French and Indians in a battle to control colonial territory.

indictment. A formal charge or accusation of a serious crime.

Intolerable Acts. Actions taken, or laws passed, that expanded the power of British authority in the colonies, specifically in response to the Boston Tea Party.

militia. A military organization of all able-bodied men during the colonial era and American Revolution who were trained to take up arms to provide for the common defense.

Minutemen. A group of men who pledged to take up arms at a minute's notice immediately before and during the American Revolution.

monopoly. An exclusive right of a person, group, or company to sell a good or product.

Sons of Liberty. Groups organized in the various colonies and formed to defend colonists' rights.

Map of the Revolutionary War Battles:

Courtesy of the National Geographic Society

Discussion Questions

1. What were Americans protesting?

   Americans were protesting the process of taxation, not the amount. Taxation without representation attacked colonists' natural rights and rights as Englishmen. Since all men are equal in their nature, they are equal in their natural rights. No man may rule another without his consent. Colonial charters guaranteed settlers the rights of Englishmen, who were protected by law against taxation without representation in Parliament.

2. What was the Boston Tea Party?

   The Boston Tea Party was a specific action meant to protest the Tea Act and the monopoly of the East India Company. Colonists dumped chests of tea into Boston Harbor.

3. Name one part of the Intolerable Acts.

   The Intolerable Acts (the colonists' name for them)
   - closed the Port of Boston;
   - replaced the government of Massachusetts with a military governor;
   - allowed British officials accused of crimes in Massachusetts to return to England for trial;
   - required Americans to be deported to England; and
   - forced the citizens of Boston to allow soldiers to live in people's private homes.

DECLARATION OF INDEPENDENCE

In Congress, July 4, 1776.

The unanimous Declaration of the thirteen united States of America,

When in the Course of human events, it becomes necessary for one people to dissolve the political bands which have connected them with another, and to assume among the powers of the earth, the separate and equal station to which the Laws of Nature and of Nature's God entitle them, a decent respect to the opinions of mankind requires that they should declare the causes which impel them to the separation.

We hold these truths to be self-evident, that all men are created equal, that they are endowed by their Creator with certain unalienable Rights, that among these are Life, Liberty and the pursuit of Happiness.—That to secure these rights, Governments are instituted among Men, deriving their just powers from the consent of the governed, That whenever any Form of Government becomes destructive of these ends, it is the Right of the People to alter or to abolish it, and to institute new Government, laying its foundation on such principles and organizing its powers in such form, as to them shall seem most likely to affect their Safety and Happiness.

Prudence, indeed, will dictate that Governments long established should not be changed for light and transient causes; and accordingly all experience hath shewn, that mankind are more disposed to suffer, while evils are sufferable, than to right themselves by abolishing the forms to which they are accustomed. But when a long train of abuses and usurpations, pursuing invariably the same Object evinces a design to reduce them under absolute Despotism, it is their right, it is their duty, to throw off such Government, and to provide new Guards for their future security.

Such has been the patient sufferance of these Colonies; and such is now the necessity which constrains them to alter their former Systems of Government. The history of the present King of Great Britain is a history of repeated injuries and usurpations, all having in direct object the establishment of an absolute Tyranny over these States. To prove this, let Facts be submitted to a candid world.

> He has refused his Assent to Laws, the most wholesome and necessary for the public good.

> He has forbidden his Governors to pass Laws of immediate and pressing importance, unless suspended in their operation till his Assent should be obtained; and when so suspended, he has utterly neglected to attend to them.

> He has refused to pass other Laws for the accommodation of large districts of people, unless those people would relinquish the right of Representation in the Legislature, a right inestimable to them and formidable to tyrants only.

> He has called together legislative bodies at places unusual, uncomfortable, and distant from the depository of their public Records, for the sole purpose of fatiguing them into compliance with his measures.

> He has dissolved Representative Houses repeatedly, for opposing with manly firmness his invasions on the rights of the people.

> He has refused for a long time, after such dissolutions, to cause others to be elected; whereby the Legislative powers, incapable of Annihilation, have returned to the People at large for their exercise; the State remaining in the mean time exposed to all the dangers of

invasion from without, and convulsions within.

He has endeavoured to prevent the population of these States; for that purpose obstructing the Laws for Naturalization of Foreigners; refusing to pass others to encourage their migrations hither, and raising the conditions of new Appropriations of Lands.

He has obstructed the Administration of Justice, by refusing his Assent to Laws for establishing Judiciary powers.

He has made Judges dependent on his Will alone, for the tenure of their offices, and the amount and payment of their salaries.

He has erected a multitude of New Offices, and sent hither swarms of Officers to harrass our people, and eat out their substance.

He has kept among us, in times of peace, Standing Armies without the Consent of our legislatures.

He has affected to render the Military independent of and superior to the Civil power.

He has combined with others to subject us to a jurisdiction foreign to our constitution, and unacknowledged by our laws; giving his Assent to their Acts of pretended legislation:

For Quartering large bodies of armed troops among us:

For protecting them, by a mock Trial, from punishment for any Murders which they should commit on the Inhabitants of these States:

For cutting off our Trade with all parts of the world:

For imposing Taxes on us without our Consent:

For depriving us in many cases, of the benefits of Trial by Jury:

For transporting us beyond Seas to be tried for pretended offences:

For abolishing the free System of English Laws in a neighbouring Province, establishing therein an Arbitrary government, and enlarging its Boundaries so as to render it at once an example and fit instrument for introducing the same absolute rule into these Colonies:

For taking away our Charters, abolishing our most valuable Laws, and altering fundamentally the Forms of our Governments:

For suspending our own Legislatures, and declaring themselves invested with power to legislate for us in all cases whatsoever.

He has abdicated Government here, by declaring us out of his Protection and waging War against us.

He has plundered our seas, ravaged our Coasts, burnt our towns, and destroyed the lives of our people.

He is at this time transporting large Armies of foreign Mercenaries to compleat the works of death, desolation and tyranny, already begun with circumstances of Cruelty & perfidy scarcely paralleled in the most barbarous ages, and totally unworthy the Head of a civilized nation.

He has constrained our fellow Citizens taken Captive on the high Seas to bear Arms against their Country, to become the executioners of their friends and Brethren, or to fall themselves by their Hands.

> He has excited domestic insurrections amongst us, and has endeavoured to bring on the inhabitants of our frontiers, the merciless Indian Savages, whose known rule of warfare, is an undistinguished destruction of all ages, sexes and conditions.

In every stage of these Oppressions We have Petitioned for Redress in the most humble terms: Our repeated Petitions have been answered only by repeated injury. A Prince whose character is thus marked by every act which may define a Tyrant, is unfit to be the ruler of a free people.

Nor have We been wanting in attentions to our British brethren. We have warned them from time to time of attempts by their legislature to extend an unwarrantable jurisdiction over us. We have reminded them of the circumstances of our emigration and settlement here.

We have appealed to their native justice and magnanimity, and we have conjured them by the ties of our common kindred to disavow these usurpations, which, would inevitably interrupt our connections and correspondence. They too have been deaf to the voice of justice and of consanguinity. We must, therefore, acquiesce in the necessity, which denounces our Separation, and hold them, as we hold the rest of mankind, Enemies in War, in Peace Friends.

We, therefore, the Representatives of the united States of America, in General Congress, Assembled, appealing to the Supreme Judge of the world for the rectitude of our intentions, do, in the Name, and by Authority of the good People of these Colonies, solemnly publish and declare, That these United Colonies are, and of Right ought to be Free and Independent States; that they are Absolved from all Allegiance to the British Crown, and that all political connection between them and the State of Great Britain, is and ought to be totally dissolved; and that as Free and Independent States, they have full Power to levy War, conclude Peace, contract Alliances, establish Commerce, and to do all other Acts and Things which Independent States may of right do.

And for the support of this Declaration, with a firm reliance on the protection of divine Providence, we mutually pledge to each other our Lives, our Fortunes and our sacred Honor.

Fifty-Six Signers of the Declaration of Independence

Georgia
Button Gwinnett
Lyman Hall
George Walton

North Carolina
William Hooper
Joseph Hewes
John Penn

South Carolina
Edward Rutledge
Thomas Heyward, Jr.
Thomas Lynch, Jr.
Arthur Middleton

Maryland
Samuel Chase
William Paca
Thomas Stone
Charles Carroll
   of Carrollton

New York
William Floyd
Philip Livingston
Francis Lewis
Lewis Morris

Virginia
George Wythe
Richard Henry Lee
Thomas Jefferson
Benjamin Harrison
Thomas Nelson, Jr.
Francis Lightfoot Lee
Carter Braxton

Pennsylvania
Robert Morris
Benjamin Rush
Benjamin Franklin
John Morton
George Clymer
James Smith
George Taylor
James Wilson
George Ross

New Jersey
Richard Stockton
John Witherspoon
Francis Hopkinson
John Hart
Abraham Clark

Delaware
Caesar Rodney
George Read
Thomas McKean

New Hampshire
Josiah Bartlett
William Whipple
Matthew Thornton

Massachusetts
Samuel Adams
John Adams
Robert Treat Paine
Elbridge Gerry
John Hancock*

Rhode Island
Stephen Hopkins
William Ellery

Connecticut
Roger Sherman
Samuel Huntington
William Williams
Oliver Wolcott

*President of the Congress

The five authors of the Declaration of Independence were Thomas Jefferson of Virginia, Roger Sherman of Connecticut, Benjamin Franklin of Pennsylvania, Robert R. Livingston of New York, and John Adams of Massachusetts. The primary author was Thomas Jefferson.

Source: The preceding text is a transcription of the Stone Engraving of the parchment Declaration of Independence (the document on display in the Rotunda at the National Archives Museum). The spelling and punctuation reflect the original.

Lesson 5

Articles of Confederation

The Union is older than the Constitution. It was formed, in fact, by the Articles of Association in 1774. It was matured and continued by the Declaration of Independence in 1776. It was further matured, and the faith of all the then thirteen States expressly plighted and engaged that it should be perpetual, by the Articles of Confederation in 1778. And finally, in 1787, one of the declared objects for ordaining and establishing the Constitution was to form a more perfect Union.

Abraham Lincoln, First Inaugural Address, March 4, 1861

Compelling Question: The first truly national government of the United States was under the Articles of Confederation. But this first constitution lasted only eight years (1781–1789). Why?

Key Concepts

1. The Thirteen Colonies needed to unite for the fight for independence, but they wanted to avoid a central government that would have too much power (like the king and Parliament of Great Britain).

2. The Articles of **Confederation** was the first **constitution** for the new federal government.

3. The goal of the Articles of Confederation was a central government that would be effective enough to fight and win the Revolution, attend to the needs of foreign policy and diplomacy, and raise just enough tax revenue to be efficient.

4. The Articles were purposefully designed to establish a **confederacy**, a form of government in which the central government would not be stronger, or have more authority, than any of the individual member states.

A New Government for a New Nation

The Battles of Lexington and Concord heralded the beginning of the American Revolutionary War in 1775. The phrase "the shot heard round the world" famously refers to the importance of the Thirteen Colonies challenging the mighty army of the King of England. The colonies were independent, and yet their leaders recognized they must work together for the common cause of fighting Great Britain. Four months after Lexington and Concord, they sent representatives to Philadelphia to form a convention called the Second Continental Congress. Peyton Randolph was elected its president, and important Founders at the Congress included Benjamin Franklin, John Adams, and Thomas Jefferson.

As discussed in Session 4, the Congress adopted the Declaration of Independence a year later to establish the new nation and logically explain and document the reasons for breaking with "mother country" Great Britain. The Continental Congress was also responsible for raising money and troops for an army, George Washington was appointed Commander of the Continental Army.

The colonists understood that they must unite if they were to survive. The delegates in Pennsylvania debated plans to unite the colonies and to create a national government that could provide for national security.

Eight days after the Declaration of Independence was adopted, John Dickinson of Pennsylvania and Delaware introduced a proposal to unify the colonies. (Each colony had a delegate; Dickinson was the principal writer.) Dickinson proposed that these "Articles of Confederation" provide for a strong central government with power to control foreign policy, raise tax revenue, resolve border disputes, and provide for national defense. But many delegates were worried that the plan would make the government too powerful.

The delegates debated how to amend the plan over the course of the next year, and in the summer of 1777, the delegates agreed on a final draft. But the Articles would not go into effect until all thirteen new states agreed. On December 16, 1777, Virginia became the first state to ratify the Articles.

While the Declaration of Independence established a new nation, the Articles of Confederation formally united the colonies into the first states and defined how they would work together as a "confederation." The confederation was a political alliance of the separate states. Each state retained its rights and authority within its boundaries. The central government (Congress) had less authority than the states. The Articles declared that the new American nation would be called "The United States of America."

Articles of Confederation

Following adoption of the Declaration of Independence, the Articles of Confederation became America's first constitution. A constitution is the supreme law of a country that establishes rules about how that country is to be governed. There are thirteen sections, or articles, in the Articles of Confederation. They provided for how the new union of thirteen states were to operate.

Many Americans were still wary of a strong central government. The tension between independent states and the central government was constant. The second article declared, "Each state retains its sovereignty, freedom, and independence, and every power, jurisdiction, and right, which is not by this Confederation expressly delegated to the United States, in Congress assembled." The main purposes of the Articles of Confederation was to unite the states to ensure their survival by providing for national defense. It gave the federal government the power to declare war. The federal government could receive ambassadors from other countries and establish a post office. Instead of national elections for a president, he was appointed for a one-year term by the delegates from the state legislatures. (Delegates served a minimum of one year with a three-year maximum.) The Articles of Confederation were established to continue into the future and could only be amended by Congress, subject to ratification by all the states.

Fighting the Revolutionary War and Afterwards

Throughout the War of Independence, General Washington struggled constantly to have enough money, materials, and men to fight the war successfully. Because the Articles of Confederation did not provide Congress with the means to raise money, the Continental Army often went hungry, and the soldiers went months (and sometimes years) without being paid. During the winter of 1777–1778, the soldiers encamped at Valley Forge, Pennsylvania. Conditions were so bad that the men often had to wrap their feet in rags because there were no shoes to be had. Men enlisting to fight for their new country were often expected to bring their own firearms because Congress wouldn't provide the funds to have muskets and bayonets manufactured.

One of the most important contributions made toward American independence was the money the French brought with them when they became allies of the new country. French supplies and arms were as important as American bravery in achieving victory at Yorktown in 1781.

In the immediate years following the defeat of the British Army until the signing of the Treaty of Paris in 1783, General Washington had to keep the Continental Army organized and intact in case fighting resumed. The continual shortage of payment and supplies almost resulted in a mutiny. The officers of the Army were ready to march on Congress and demand their back pay. Only the swift and decisive leadership of General Washington averted what would have been a disaster had the mutiny actually occurred.

The Articles of Confederation: A Failure or a Beginning?

The events of the War of Independence revealed that the Articles of Confederation were too weak a constitution to hold thirteen strong-willed and independent-minded states together in a single effective union once the common threat posed by the British Army had been removed. The Articles of Confederation were ineffective because they did not provide a strong president. The one-year term did not allow continuity of leadership. There was no power to enforce laws or assess taxes to pay for government expenses. This was revealed even before the Articles were ratified and went into full effect in 1781.

As will be explored in the following activity, under the Articles of Confederation, the United States Congress was able to address the competing land claims of the various former colonies to territories west of the existing thirteen states. Also, the most significant legislation enacted under the Articles of Confederation was the Northwest Ordinance of 1787, which is one of the four **"Organic Laws of the United States."** (See Session 6.)

To be fair, the Articles of Confederation was flawed, but it was not a complete failure. Although it did not provide the necessary organization and structure to ensure the long-term success of the newly independent United States, the Articles of Confederation was a necessary step in the right direction. The Founders made a true and authentic effort to find the right balance between the authoritarian actions of King George and the British Parliament and the sincere desires of each new state within the union to enjoy the fullest measure of freedom possible. In 1789, the U.S. Constitution took effect, replacing the Articles of Confederation and instituting a better way to govern the United States.

■ Key Terms

confederacy, or **confederation.** A form of united government under which the member states retain a higher degree of authority over themselves, while the central authority (Congress) has a lesser degree of authority over the states as a group.

constitution. The supreme (ultimate) law of a country that establishes written rules about how a country is to be governed.

Organic Laws of the United States. Also known as "Organic Laws," they are the formal laws that establish the permanent and general laws of the United States. These are:
1. Declaration of Independence
2. Articles of Confederation
3. U.S. Constitution, including the Bill of Rights (Amendments I through X)
4. Northwest Ordinance of 1787.

Land Claims of the First States under the Articles of Confederation

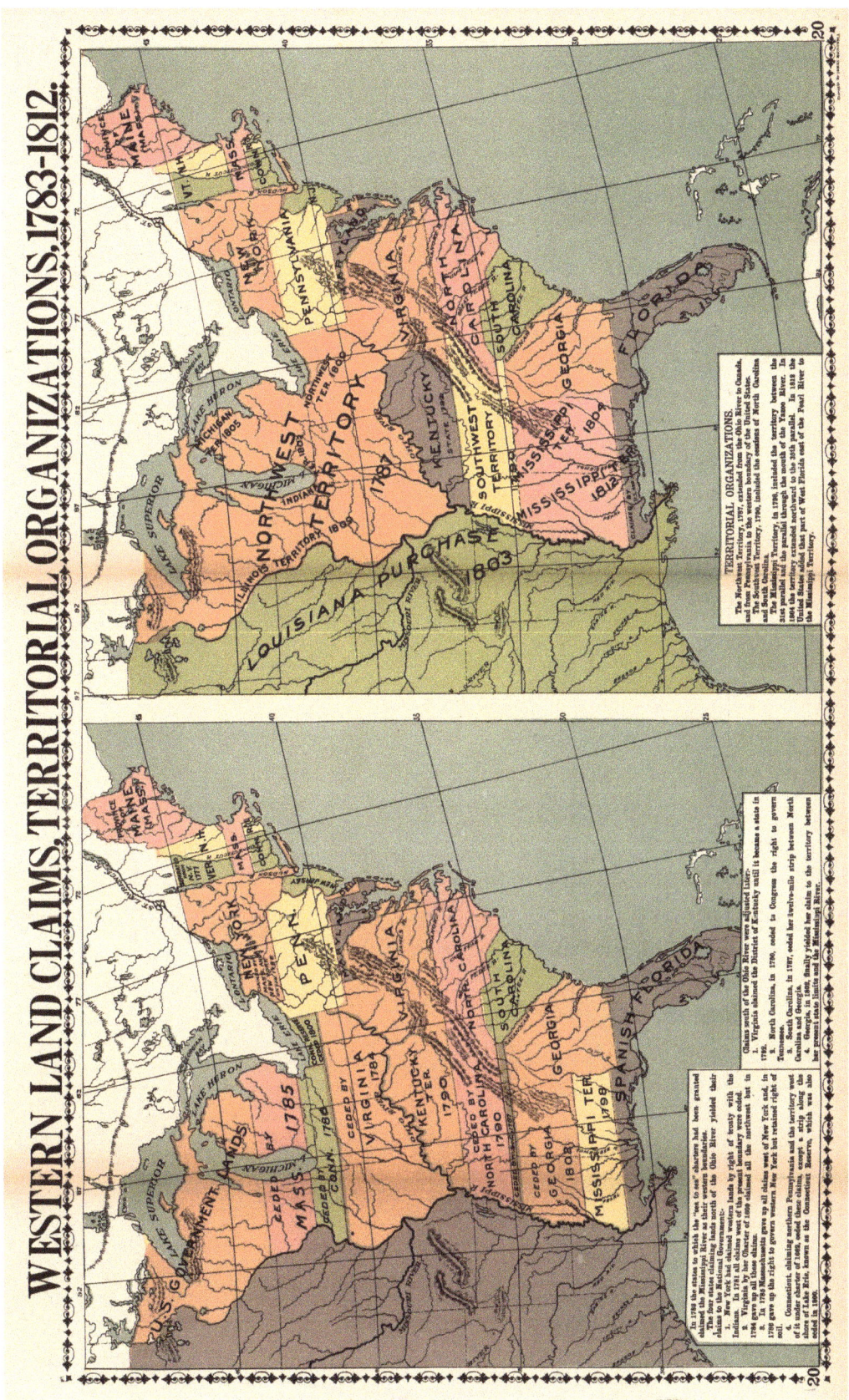

Library of Congress, Geography and Map Division.

LESSON FIVE | 43

Discussion Questions

1. The First Continental Congress drafted the Declaration of Independence, which explained to the world why the American people had the right to form a new, independent nation.

2. Why did the Founders want to unite the Thirteen Colonies into one nation?

   The Thirteen Colonies needed a national government to act on behalf of all of the colonies, especially in addressing the challenges of fighting a war with Great Britain. The Americans seeking independence understood that their new nation could not survive if it were to remain separated into thirteen independent states. Therefore, the delegates in Pennsylvania also started to discuss a plan to unite the states and to create a national government that could provide for national security.

3. Why was the plan to unite the Thirteen States called the "Articles of Confederation?" What is a confederacy?

   This new plan was called the "Articles of Confederation" because the Thirteen States united into a confederation of sovereign states that would still have their own governments that could pass their own laws. The Articles declared that the new American nation would be a "confederacy" called "The United States of America." It was a confederacy because the states had greater individual authority than the central government within the state boundaries than the authority of the central government.

4. Why was the new American nation called "The United States of America"?

   The Thirteen Colonies united into a confederation of sovereign states that would still have their own governments that could pass their own laws. The Articles declared that the new American nation would be a confederacy called "The United States of America."

5. The Articles of Confederation was established at the Second Continental Congress.

6. The Articles of Confederation was the first U.S. constitution.

7. Virginia was the first state to ratify the Articles of Confederation.

8. The Articles of Confederation united Thirteen Colonies as sovereign states with their own state governments.

9. The Articles declared that the new American nation would be a confederacy called "The United States of America."

10. What were the ADVANTAGES for each state in settling the Western Land Claims? (Answers may vary.)

    Only a simple majority of states was needed to make a decision. Each state was fully sovereign (all states equal). Each state's claim was based on old British land grants (which could not be appealed).

11. What were the DISADVANTAGES for each state in settling the Western Land Claims? (Answers may vary.)

    Competing states had to convince a majority of the other states to support their claim. Each state was fully sovereign. The size of a state (in land or in population) was not reflected. There was no chief executive (king or president) or courts to mediate disagreements.

ARTICLES OF CONFEDERATION AND PERPETUAL UNION

Adopted by the Continental Congress November 15, 1777
Ratified by the 13 States March 1, 1781

To all to whom these Presents shall come, we, the undersigned Delegates of the States affixed to our Names send greeting. Whereas the Delegates of the United States of America in Congress assembled did on the fifteenth day of November in the year of our Lord One Thousand Seven Hundred and Seventy seven, and in the Second Year of the Independence of America agree to certain articles of Confederation and perpetual Union between the States of New Hampshire, Massachusetts-bay, Rhode Island and Providence Plantations, Connecticut, New York, New Jersey, Pennsylvania, Delaware, Maryland, Virginia, North Carolina, South Carolina, and Georgia in the Words following, viz. Articles of Confederation and perpetual Union between the States of New Hampshire, Massachusetts-bay, Rhode Island and Providence Plantations, Connecticut, New York, New Jersey, Pennsylvania, Delaware, Maryland, Virginia, North Carolina, South Carolina, and Georgia.

Article I. The Stile of this confederacy shall be, "The United States of America."

Article II. Each state retains its sovereignty, freedom and independence, and every Power, Jurisdiction and right, which is not by this confederation expressly delegated to the United States, in Congress assembled.

Article III. The said states hereby severally enter into a firm league of friendship with each other, for their common defense, the security of their Liberties, and their mutual and general welfare, binding themselves to assist each other, against all force offered to, or attacks made upon them, or any of them, on account of religion, sovereignty, trade, or any other pretence whatever.

Article IV. The better to secure and perpetuate mutual friendship and intercourse among the people of the different states in this union, the free inhabitants of each of these states, paupers, vagabonds and fugitives from Justice excepted, shall be entitled to all privileges and immunities of free citizens in the several states; and the people of each state shall have free ingress and regress to and from any other state, and shall enjoy therein all the privileges of trade and commerce, subject to the same duties, impositions and restrictions as the inhabitants thereof respectively, provided that such restrictions shall not extend so far as to prevent the removal of property imported into any state, to any other State of which the Owner is an inhabitant; provided also that no imposition, duties or restriction shall be laid by any state, on the property of the united states, or either of them.

If any Person guilty of, or charged with, treason, felony, or other high misdemeanor in any state, shall flee from Justice, and be found in any of the united states, he shall upon demand of the Governor or executive power of the state from which he fled, be delivered up, and removed to the state having jurisdiction of his offence.

Full faith and credit shall be given in each of these states to the records, acts and judicial proceedings of the courts and magistrates of every other state.

Article V. For the more convenient management of the general interests of the united states, delegates shall be annually appointed in such manner as the legislature of each state shall direct, to meet in Congress on the first Monday in November, in every year, with a power reserved to each state to recall its delegates, or any of them, at any time within the year, and to send others in their stead, for the remainder of the Year. No State shall be represented in Congress by less than two, nor by more than seven Members; and no person shall be capable of being delegate for more than three years, in any term of six years; nor shall any person, being a delegate, be capable of holding any office under the united states, for which he, or another for his benefit receives any salary, fees or emolument of any kind.

Each State shall maintain its own delegates in a meeting of the states, and while they act as members of the committee of the states.

In determining questions in the united states, in Congress assembled, each state shall have one vote.

Freedom of speech and debate in Congress shall not be impeached or questioned in any Court, or place out of Congress, and the members of congress shall be protected in their persons from arrests and imprisonments, during the time of their going to and from, and attendance on congress, except for treason, felony, or breach of the peace.

Article VI. No State, without the Consent of the united States, in congress assembled, shall send any embassy to, or receive any embassy from, or enter into any conference, agreement, alliance, or treaty, with any King, prince or state; nor shall any person holding any office of profit or trust under the united states, or any of them, accept of any present, emolument, office, or title of any kind whatever, from any King, prince, or foreign state; nor shall the united states, in congress assembled, or any of them, grant any title of nobility.

No two or more states shall enter into any treaty, confederation, or alliance whatever between them, without the consent of the united states, in congress assembled, specifying accurately the purposes for which the same is to be entered into, and how long it shall continue.

No State shall lay any imposts or duties, which may interfere with any stipulations in treaties, entered into by the united States in congress assembled, with any King, prince, or State, in pursuance of any treaties already proposed by congress, to the courts of France and Spain.

No vessels of war shall be kept up in time of peace, by any state, except such number only, as shall be deemed necessary by the united states, in congress assembled, for the defense of such state, or its trade; nor shall any body of forces be kept up, by any state, in time of peace, except such number only as, in the judgment of the united states, in congress assembled, shall be deemed requisite to garrison the forts necessary for the defense of such state; but every state shall always keep up a well regulated and disciplined militia, sufficiently armed and accoutered, and shall provide and constantly have ready for use, in public stores, a due number of field pieces and tents, and a proper quantity of arms, ammunition, and camp equipage.

No State shall engage in any war without the consent of the united States in congress assembled, unless such State be actually invaded by enemies, or shall have received certain advice of a resolution being formed by some nation of Indians to invade such State, and the danger is so imminent as not to admit of a delay till the united states in congress assembled, can be consulted: nor shall any state grant commissions to any ships or vessels of war, nor letters of marque or reprisal, except it be after a declaration of war by the united states in congress assembled, and then only against the kingdom or State, and the subjects thereof, against which war has been so declared, and under such regulations as shall be established by the united states in congress assembled, unless such state be infested by pirates, in which case vessels of war may be fitted out for that occasion, and kept so long as the danger shall continue, or until the united states in congress assembled shall determine otherwise.

Article VII. When land forces are raised by any state, for the common defense, all officers of or under the rank of colonel, shall be appointed by the legislature of each state respectively by whom such forces shall be raised, or in such manner as such state shall direct, and all vacancies shall be filled up by the state which first made appointment.

Article VIII. All charges of war, and all other expenses that shall be incurred for the common defense or general welfare, and allowed by the united states in congress assembled, shall be defrayed out of a common treasury, which shall be supplied by the several states, in proportion to the value of all land within each state, granted to or surveyed for any Person, as such land and the buildings and improvements thereon shall be estimated, according to such mode as the united states, in congress assembled, shall, from time to time, direct and appoint. The taxes for paying that proportion shall be laid and levied by the authority and direction of the legislatures of the several states within the time agreed upon by the united states in congress assembled.

Article IX. The united states, in congress assembled, shall have the sole and exclusive right and power of determining on peace and war, except in the cases mentioned in the sixth article—of sending and receiving ambassadors—entering into treaties and alliances, provided that no treaty of commerce shall be made, whereby the legislative power of the respective states shall be restrained from imposing such imposts and duties on foreigners, as their own people are subjected to, or from prohibiting the exportation or importation of any species of goods or commodities whatsoever—of establishing rules for deciding, in all cases, what captures on land or water shall be legal, and in what manner prizes taken by land or naval forces in the service of the united Sates, shall be divided or appropriated—of granting letters of marque and reprisal in times of peace—appointing courts for the trial of piracies and felonies committed on the high seas; and establishing courts; for receiving and determining finally appeals in all cases of captures, provided that no member of congress shall be appointed a judge of any of the said courts.

The united states, in congress assembled, shall also be the last resort on appeal, in all disputes and differences now subsisting, or that hereafter may arise between two or more states concerning boundary, jurisdiction, or any other cause whatever; which authority shall always be exercised in the manner following. Whenever the legislative or executive authority, or lawful agent of any state in controversy with another, shall present a petition to congress, stating the matter in question, and praying for a hearing, notice thereof shall be given, by order of congress, to the legislative or executive authority of the other state in controversy, and a day assigned for the appearance of the parties by their lawful agents, who shall then be directed to appoint, by joint consent, commissioners or judges to constitute a court for hearing and determining the matter in question: but if they cannot agree, congress shall name three persons out of each of the united states, and from the list of such persons each party shall alternately strike out one, the petitioners beginning, until the number shall be reduced to thirteen; and from that number not less than seven, nor more than nine names, as congress shall direct, shall, in the presence of congress, be drawn out by lot, and the persons whose names shall be so drawn, or any five of them, shall be commissioners or judges, to hear and finally determine the controversy, so always as a major part of the judges, who shall hear the cause, shall agree in the determination: and if either party shall neglect to attend at the day appointed, without showing reasons which congress shall judge sufficient, or being present, shall refuse to strike, the congress shall proceed to nominate three persons out of each State, and the secretary of congress shall strike in behalf of such party absent or refusing; and the judgment and sentence of the court, to be appointed in the manner before prescribed, shall be final and conclusive; and if any of the parties shall refuse to submit to the authority of such court, or to appear or defend their claim or cause, the court shall nevertheless proceed to pronounce sentence, or judgment, which shall in like manner be final and decisive; the judgment or sentence and other proceedings being in either case transmitted to congress, and lodged among the acts of congress, for the security of the parties concerned: provided that every commissioner, before he sits in judgment, shall take an oath to be administered by one of the judges of the supreme or superior court of the State where the cause shall be tried, "well and truly to hear and determine the matter in question, according to the best of his judgment, without favour, affection, or hope of reward:" provided, also, that no State shall be deprived of territory for the benefit of the united states.

All controversies concerning the private right of soil claimed under different grants of two or more states, whose jurisdictions as they may respect such lands, and the states which passed such grants are adjusted, the said grants or either of them being at the same time claimed to have originated antecedent to such settlement of jurisdiction, shall, on the petition of either party to the congress of the united states, be finally determined, as near as may be, in the same manner as is before prescribed for deciding disputes respecting territorial jurisdiction between different states.

The united states, in congress assembled, shall also have the sole and exclusive right and power of regulating the alloy and value of coin struck by their own authority, or by that of the respective states—fixing the standard of weights and measures throughout the united states—regulating the trade and managing all affairs with the Indians, not members of any of the states; provided that the legislative right of any state, within its own limits, be not infringed or violated—establishing and regulating post-offices from one state to another, throughout all the united states, and exacting such postage on the papers passing through the same, as may be requisite to defray the expenses of the said office—appointing all officers of the land forces in the service of the united States, excepting regimental officers—appointing all the officers of the naval forces, and commissioning all officers whatever in the service of the united states—making rules for the government and regulation of the said land and naval forces, and directing their operations.

The united states, in congress assembled, shall have authority to appoint a committee, to sit in the recess of congress, to be denominated, "A Committee of the States," and to consist of one delegate from each State; and to appoint such other committees and civil officers as may be necessary for managing the general affairs of the united states under their direction—to appoint one of their number to preside; provided that no person be allowed to serve in the office of president more than one year in any term of three years; to ascertain the necessary sums of money to be raised for the service of the united states, and to appropriate and apply the same for defraying the public expenses—to borrow money or emit bills on the credit of the united states, transmitting every half year to the respective states an account of the sums of money so borrowed or emitted—to build and equip a navy—to agree upon the number of land forces, and to make requisitions from each state for its quota, in proportion to the number of white inhabitants in such state, which requisition shall be binding; and thereupon the legislature of each state shall appoint the regimental officers, raise the men, and clothe, arm, and equip them, in a soldier-like manner, at the expense of the united states; and the officers and men so clothed, armed, and equipped, shall march to the place appointed, and within the time agreed on by the united states, in congress assembled; but if the united states, in congress assembled, shall, on consideration of circumstances, judge proper that any state should not raise men, or should raise a smaller number than its quota, and that any other state should raise a greater number of men than the quota thereof, such extra number shall be raised, officered, clothed, armed, and equipped in the same manner as the quota of such state, unless the legislature of such state shall judge that such extra number cannot be safely spared out of the same, in which case they shall raise, officer, clothe, arm, and equip, as many of such extra number as they judge can be safely spared. And the officers and men so clothed, armed, and equipped, shall march to the place appointed, and within the time agreed on by the united states in congress assembled.

The united states, in congress assembled, shall never engage in a war, nor grant letters of marque and reprisal in time of peace, nor enter into any treaties or alliances, nor coin money, nor regulate the value thereof nor ascertain the sums and expenses necessary for the defence and welfare of the united states, or any of them, nor emit bills, nor borrow money on the credit of the united states, nor appropriate money, nor agree upon the number of vessels of war to be built or purchased, or the number of land or sea forces to be raised, nor appoint a commander in chief of the army or navy, unless nine states assent to the same, nor shall a question on any other point, except for adjourning from day to day, be determined, unless by the votes of a majority of the united states in congress assembled.

The Congress of the united states shall have power to adjourn to any time within the year, and to any place within the united states, so that no period of adjournment be for a longer duration than the space of six Months, and shall publish the Journal of their proceedings monthly, except such parts thereof relating to treaties, alliances, or military operations, as in their judgment require secrecy; and the yeas and nays of the delegates of each State, on any question, shall be entered on the Journal, when it is desired by any delegate; and the delegates of a State, or any of them, at his or their request, shall be furnished with a transcript of the said Journal, except such parts as are above excepted, to lay before the legislatures of the several states.

Article X. The committee of the states, or any nine of them, shall be authorized to execute, in the recess of congress, such of the powers of congress as the united states, in congress assembled, by the consent of nine states, shall, from time to time, think expedient to vest them with; provided that no power be delegated to the said committee, for the exercise of which, by the articles of confederation, the voice of nine states, in the congress of the united states assembled, is requisite.

Article XI. Canada acceding to this confederation, and joining in the measures of the united states, shall be admitted into, and entitled to all the advantages of this union: but no other Colony shall be admitted into the same, unless such admission be agreed to by nine states.

Article XII. All bills of credit emitted, monies borrowed, and debts contracted by or under the authority of congress, before the assembling of the united states, in pursuance of the present confederation, shall be deemed and considered as a charge against the united states, for payment and satisfaction whereof the said united states and the public faith are hereby solemnly pledged.

Article XIII. Every State shall abide by the determinations of the united states, in congress assembled, on all questions which by this confederation are submitted to them. And the Articles of this confederation shall be inviolably observed by every state, and the union shall be perpetual; nor shall any alteration at any time hereafter be made in any of them, unless such alteration be agreed to in a congress of the united states, and be afterwards con-firmed by the legislatures of every state.

And Whereas it hath pleased the Great Governor of the World to incline the hearts of the legislatures we respectively represent in congress, to approve of, and to authorize us to ratify the said articles of confederation and perpetual union, Know Ye, that we, the undersigned delegates, by virtue of the power and authority to us given for that purpose, do, by these presents, in the name and in behalf of our respective constituents, fully and entirely ratify and confirm each and every of the said articles of confederation and perpetual union, and all and singular the matters and things therein contained. And we do further solemnly plight and engage the faith of our respective constituents, that they shall abide by the determinations of the united states in congress assembled, on all questions, which by the said confederation are submitted to them. And that the articles thereof shall be inviolably observed by the states we respectively represent, and that the union shall be perpetual.

In Witness whereof, we have hereunto set our hands, in Congress. Done at Philadelphia, in the State of Pennsylvania, the ninth Day of July, in the Year of our Lord one Thousand seven Hundred and Seventy eight, and in the third year of the Independence of America.

Andrew Adams, Connecticut, Lawyer	Edward Langworthy, Georgia, Teacher
Samuel Adams, Massachusetts, Merchant	Henry Laurens, South Carolina, Merchant
Thomas Adams, Virginia, Businessman	Francis Lightfoot Lee, Virginia, Planter
John Banister, Virginia, Businessman	Richard H. Lee, Virginia, Planter/Merchant
Josiah Bartlett, New Hampshire, Physician	Francis Lewis, New York, Merchant
Daniel Carroll, Maryland, Farmer	James Lovell, Massachusetts, Teacher
William Clingan, Pennsylvania, Judge	Henry Marchant, Rhode Island, Lawyer
John Collins, Rhode Island, Lawyer	John Mathews, South Carolina, Lawyer
Francis Dana, Massachusetts, Lawyer	Thomas McKean, Delaware, Lawyer
John Dickinson, Delaware, Lawyer	Gouvernour Morris, New York, Lawyer
William H. Drayton, South Carolina, Lawyer	Robert Morris, Pennsylvania, Merchant
James Duane, New York, Judge	John Penn, North Carolina, Lawyer
William Duer, New York, Judge	Joseph Reed, Pennsylvania, Lawyer
William Ellery, Rhode Island, Merchant	Daniel Roberdeau, Pennsylvania, Merchant
Elbridge Gerry, Massachusetts, Merchant	Nathaniel Scudder, New Jersey, Doctor
John Hancock, Massachusetts, Merchant	Roger Sherman, Connecticut, Lawyer
John Hanson, Maryland, Merchant	Jonathan B. Smith, Pennsylvania, Merchant
Cornelius Harnett, North Carolina, Farmer	Edward Telfair, Georgia, Merchant
John Harvie, Virginia, Lawyer	Nicholas Van Dyke, Delaware, Lawyer
Thomas Heyward, Jr., South Carolina, Planter	John Walton, Georgia, Planter
Samuel Holten, Massachusetts, Doctor	John Wentworth, Jr., New Hampshire, Lawyer
Titus Hosmer, Connecticut, Lawyer	John Williams, North Carolina, Soldier
Samuel Huntington, Connecticut, Lawyer	John Witherspoon, New Jersey, Minister
Richard Hutson, South Carolina, Lawyer	Oliver Wolcott, Connecticut, Lawyer

Lesson 6

Northwest Ordinance of 1787

There was nothing said in the Constitution relative to the spread of slavery in the Territories, but the same generation of men said something about it in this [Northwest] ordinance of [17]87, through the influence of which you of Indiana, and your neighbors in Ohio, Illinois, Wisconsin and Michigan, are prosperous, free men. . . . Our fathers [Founders] who made the government, made the ordinance of 1787.

Abraham Lincoln, Indianapolis, Indiana, 1859

Compelling Question: The Articles of Confederation was the first constitution of the United States, yet it lasted only eight years. A major accomplishment under the Articles of Confederation was the adoption of the Northwest Ordinance of 1787. What is the lasting significance of this organic law for the future of the United States?

Key Concepts

1. The Northwest Ordinance of 1787 was produced under the Articles of Confederation, and it was passed by the thirteen states (including free and slave).

2. The ordinance created a regular and consistent process for new states to be established and organized, and then to join the federal union as equals with the original states.

3. The ordinance also set rules respecting the rights of Indian nations living within the Northwest Territory.

4. The Northwest Ordinance established strict prohibitions against the expansion of slavery into new states.

5. It set the precedent that the national government had the authority to provide oversight and constrain or restrict slavery as an institution within the country as a whole.

The Least Known of the Founding Documents

The Northwest Ordinance was adopted by the Confederation Congress (under the Articles of Confederation) just two months before adoption of the U.S. Constitution, by a vote of 17 to 1. This little-known organic law was key to the founding of the United States of America. The most important contributions to the United States were (1) establishing a system of courts and government for the Northwest Territory; (2) an orderly way to add states to the union; (3) guarantee of the freedom of contract and private property rights; (4) outlawing slavery in the Northwest Territory that would eventually become five states; and (5) addressing the abuse of Native Americans and properly paying them for their properties.

The four **Organic (founding) Laws of the United States** are closely linked. They all advanced the cause of freedom and natural rights. This is because many of the Founders who signed the Declaration of Independence also participated in the Revolutionary War. And many of them wrote, voted for, or signed the Articles of Confederation, the Northwest Ordinance, or the Constitution. The Northwest Ordinance of 1787 is the least known of the founding documents. But it played a major role in American history and the advance of freedom.

Under the Articles of Confederation, Congress enacted ordinances in 1784, 1785, and 1787 that established the framework for expansion of the United States in the regions north and west of the Ohio River. The Land Ordinance of 1784, written by Thomas Jefferson, set up a court system for a territorial government. But it was replaced in 1785 and further revised. The resulting Northwest Ordinance of 1787 established how public lands would be sold to private interests and provided for new states.

Rufus King and Nathan Dane, Massachusetts Delegates to the Confederation Congress, wrote the Northwest Ordinance of 1787. Rufus King was also a delegate to the Constitutional Convention that same summer.

The Northwest Territory

The 1783 Treaty of Paris marked the official end of the hard-fought Revolutionary War and brought peace between Great Britain and the new United States of America. The treaty granted the Northwest Territory to the victorious Americans.

People today might confuse the Northwest Territory with the Northwest Territories in Canada or the Pacific Northwest. But in 1783, the Northwest Territory was in the area we now call the "Midwest." It was bordered on the west by the upper Mississippi River, on the east by Pennsylvania, on the south and southwest by the Ohio River, and on the north by the Great Lakes and Canada.

Westward Expansion and States' Land Claims

As settlers moved west past the borders of the original states, the governments of Connecticut, Massachusetts, Virginia, New York, North Carolina, South Carolina, and Georgia sought to add more land to their states. (See Session 5 for a discussion of the land claims by the states.)

Under the Articles of Confederation, on July 13, 1787, the Confederation Congress passed the Northwest Ordinance of 1787. The Northwest Ordinance was the greatest accomplishment of the new country under the Articles of Confederation. The ordinance barred existing states from extending their borders, which ended the land claims disputes and provided for the orderly growth of the nation.

The ordinance also established the federal government's authority over the states. Congress (not the states) was granted the right to govern the Northwest Territory and set the rules for how new states would enter the Confederation (later the federal union). Congress, too, had the right to divide the Northwest Territory into three to five smaller territories, which would eventually become states.

By offering free land, the ordinance encouraged settlers to move to the new territory. When 5,000 free men moved to one of the divisions, they gained the right to self-government. When the population reached 60,000 free inhabitants, they would be entitled to draft their own **republican** government and constitution and petition Congress for statehood. The new state would be admitted to the union "on an equal footing with the original states." This process established a legal **precedent** for how new states would be added to the union.

Eventually, the states of Ohio, Indiana, Illinois, Michigan, Wisconsin, and a part of Minnesota entered the union from the Northwest Territory. They were granted full equality with the thirteen original states.

A key aspect of the Northwest Ordinance was the establishment of fee simple ownership, by which a person could purchase land and own it permanently with unlimited power to sell it, give it away, or leave it to his or her children. This has been called "the first guarantee of freedom of contract in the United States."

In 1789, the newly ratified U.S. Constitution established a stronger federal government. Congress reaffirmed its support of the Northwest Ordinance of 1787 with slight changes under the new Constitution. President George Washington signed the ordinance in 1789. The ordinance was to "be considered as articles of compact between the original States and the people and states in the said territory, and forever remain unalterable, unless by common consent." In other words, the ordinance was not ordinary legislation that Congress could amend.

Advance of Freedom and Natural Rights

The Northwest Ordinance, also known as the "Freedom Ordinance," echoed the call for liberty in the Declaration of Independence and legally affirmed the natural rights of all people in the Northwest Territory. Among these rights were freedom of religion; freedom from oppressive government; rights of those accused of a crime, including trial by jury; protection of private property; and rights of contract and inheritance. These rights were later included in the Constitution and the Bill of Rights.

Education based on "religion, morality, and knowledge" was encouraged in the Northwest Ordinance because they are "necessary to good government and the happiness of mankind." Land was set aside in each township for schools. Eventually, this led to federal funding to develop a public-school system in the territory. (See Section 14, Article 3.) By passing the Northwest Ordinance, the Founders made their first attempt to stop the spread of slavery by federal law. Article 6, the most famous article, provided that "there shall never be slavery nor involuntary servitude in the said territory" and any new states in the Northwest Territory joining the union. Rufus King and Nathan Dane, the two authors of the Northwest Ordinance of 1787, strongly opposed slavery. Their words highlighted the thinking of most of the Founders, which is why the ordinance passed 17 to 1. This ordinance created a natural dividing line between free and slave states at the Ohio River. (See Section 14, Article 6.)

When Abraham Lincoln was running for U.S. president, he mentioned the Northwest Ordinance as evidence that the federal government could regulate slavery. During a speech in Indianapolis, Indiana, in 1859, Lincoln indicated that President Washington and other Founders approved banning slavery in the Northwest Territory with these words:

> *There was nothing said in the Constitution relative to the spread of slavery in the Territories, but the same generation of men said something about it in this [Northwest] ordinance of [17]87, through the influence of which you of Indiana, and your neighbors in Ohio, Illinois, Wisconsin and Michigan, are prosperous, free men. . . . Our fathers [Founders] who made the government, made the ordinance of 1787.*

Founders' Attempts to Abolish Slavery and Abuse of Indians

Though the Founders could not unite all thirteen states to fight the War of Independence and simultaneously eliminate slavery, they resolved to stop its spread into territories and new states. They succeeded in preventing slavery in the Northwest Territory by passing the Northwest Ordinance of 1787, Section 14, Article 6. (See Session 7 for more in-depth coverage about slavery.)

The Founders were also aware that Native Americans, then known as "Indians," faced discrimination and abuse. Because of this mistreatment, the Founders addressed Indian property, rights, and liberty in the Northwest Ordinance (Section 14, Article 3):

> *The utmost good faith shall always be observed towards the Indians; their lands and property shall never be taken from them without their consent; and, in their property, rights, and liberty, they shall never be invaded or disturbed, unless in just and lawful wars authorized by Congress; but laws founded in justice and humanity, shall from time to time be made for preventing wrongs being done to them, and for preserving peace and friendship with them.*

Unfortunately, the Founders' good intentions did not stop the federal government from taking Indian lands, forcing them to move from their homes to live on reservations, and discriminating against them in courts, jails, employment, and voting rights. As settlers and the U.S. military moved westward, Indians often (and understandably) fiercely resisted. Both sides fought in self-defense and also committed atrocities.

In the early Americas, diseases were rampant without modern vaccinations against smallpox, measles, diphtheria, typhus, and the like. All races suffered and died from them. Indians were particularly susceptible to the diseases because they had no natural immunity. Death estimates range up to tens of millions resulting from disease brought by infected European explorers and settlers and African slaves.

As of January 2022, the federal Bureau of Indian Affairs (BIA) has recognized 574 sovereign tribal nations. The BIA (formerly the Office of Indian Affairs) was created in 1824 to address health concerns and many other issues. A quarter of the four to five million Native Americans and Alaska Natives live on 326 federally protected Indian reservations. Occupying more than 56 million acres of land, the reservations are held in trust by the United States for the tribes. While the reservation system has encouraged the preservation of Native American community, culture, and history, many sociologists have noted that the lack of private property on reservations has caused them a host of problems, such as low rates of economic development and poverty.

Over time, the culture of freedom and recognition that all Americans must be treated equally under the law resulted in outlawing slavery (Amendment XIII) and many laws to correct abuse of Native Americans. These laws include Cherokee Indians being recognized as U.S. citizens in 1817; the first Civil Rights Act of 1866; adoption of the Constitutional Amendment XIV in 1868; the Indian Citizenship Act in 1924; the Civil Rights Act of 1964; the Voting Rights Act of 1965; the Indian Civil Rights Act of 1968; the Alaska Native Claims Settlement Act of 1971; and the American Indian Religious Freedom Act of 1978.

While the list of abuses and discrimination among all races is long, there have always been positive relationships as well. From the founding of the colonies to the present, cooperation, friendship, and intermarriage have occurred among Indians and whites. Important historical examples include Squanto's assisting the Pilgrims to survive; Pocahontas's saving Captain John Smith's life and marriage to John Rolfe; and Sacajawea's guiding the Lewis and Clark Expedition. In the Revolutionary War and all U.S wars since, Native Americans, blacks, and whites have fought together for the cause of freedom. Today, three-fourths of Native Americans live within American society. Many whites have traces of Native American ancestry. Substantial progress in racial acceptance and rights for all has occurred.

We must always seek virtue, and we must do good to all people. President Abraham Lincoln, in his first inaugural address in 1861, challenged all Americans with these words:

We must not be enemies. Though passion may have strained, it must not break our bonds of affection. The mystic chords of memory, stretching from every battlefield and patriot grave to every living heart and hearthstone all over this broad land, will yet swell the chorus of the Union, when touched again, as surely they will be, by the better angels of our nature.

■ Key Terms

fee simple ownership. Ownership that gives property owners the right to fully enjoy their buildings and property, except when restricted by zoning, government taking of property by eminent domain, deed or subdivision requirements, or covenants. It is the most common type of real estate ownership in the United States.

involuntary servitude. A form of labor in which a person is forced to work against his or her will for the benefit of someone else. Amendment XIII abolished involuntary servitude.

ordinance. An authoritative government decree, rule, or law.

Organic Laws of the United States. The founding documents of the U.S. government. The U.S. Code includes four Organic Laws: the Declaration of Independence, the Articles of Confederation, the Northwest Ordinance of 1787, and the U.S. Constitution with the Bill of Rights, Amendments 1 through 10.

precedent. A principle in law that uses a past legal decision to help interpret and decide a current case.

republican. Relating to the form of government of all states in the United States and its federal government in which the people elect the executive and legislative officials to represent them.

territory. A part of the United States (or other country) not included within any state (or government division) but organized with a separate governing body.

Discussion Questions

1. What was the significance of the Northwest Ordinance of 1787? What did it accomplish?

   The Northwest Ordinance was significant because it established the precedent for new states to join the union by an orderly process. Once new areas were populated, they could petition Congress to join as new states with the same rights as citizens in the original states. Also, articles in the Northwest Ordinance recognized that the property rights of Indians should be respected and that slavery would be banned in the states created from the Northwest Territory.

2. How did the Northwest Ordinance of 1787 help resolve the competing western land claims of the states between 1783 and 1789?

   Seven of the original states saw an opportunity to expand their borders westward. But the adoption of the Northwest Ordinance ended their efforts and established a process for the creation of new states out of land in the West.

3. What were the five new states that eventually joined the United States as a result of the Northwest Ordinance?

   Ohio, Indiana, Illinois, Michigan, and Wisconsin. Also, a part of Minnesota.

4. What is the relationship between the Northwest Ordinance, the Declaration of Independence, the Articles of Confederation, and the Constitution?

   The Declaration of Independence is the foundational document of the country, establishing that our rights as citizens are not granted by the state, but by our Creator, and that it is the duty of the state to protect those rights. The Northwest Ordinance was a major accomplishment under the Articles of Confederation. It was a key in the development of the United States in that it established precedents and rules and regulations on how areas of America could join the original thirteen states as new states with equal protection of rights. It was the first federal document with language protecting the rights of Indians and preventing slavery in the Northwest Territory. The U.S. Constitution was the final charter of the nation that resulted from the Constitutional Convention in Philadelphia, producing the framework that would allow proper governance of the states. The first ten amendments to the U.S. Constitution, known as "the Bill of Rights," were added to make sure that the government would respect the individual rights of citizens.

5. What are the four organic (founding) laws that created the United States of America?

   The Declaration of Independence (1776); the Articles of Confederation (approved by the Continental Congress in 1777 and ratified by the original 13 states in 1781); the Northwest Ordinance of 1787; and the U.S. Constitution (adopted by Congress in 1787, ratified by the states in 1788, and amended with the Bill of Rights ratified in 1791).

6. What part did "virtue" play in the eventual elimination of slavery and correcting abuse of Native Americans?

The history of the world includes an unending list of examples of "man's inhumanity to man." Slavery, involuntary servitude, murder, total domination of people by power-hungry rulers, abuse of property rights (including stealing), and denial of God-given "natural rights" are prime examples. The Founders had a deep and abiding respect for Judeo-Christian ethics and morals, and this foundation set the stage for eliminating inhumane, institutions, including slavery. Yet it also took much time for enough Americans to reject age-old prejudices and to advocate changing laws through their elected representatives. In the end, virtue can overcome evil if citizens act on their civic duty.

NORTHWEST ORDINANCE of 1787

July 13, 1787
An Ordinance for the government of the Territory of the United States northwest of the River Ohio

Adopted by the Congress of the Confederation of the United States
Reaffirmed by the new Congress August 7, 1789

Section 1. Be it ordained by the United States in Congress assembled, That the said territory, for the purposes of temporary government, be one district, subject, however, to be divided into two districts, as future circumstances may, in the opinion of Congress, make it expedient.

Section 2. Be it ordained by the authority aforesaid, That the estates, both of resident and nonresident proprietors in the said territory, dying intestate, shall descent to, and be distributed among their children, and the descendants of a deceased child, in equal parts; the descendants of a deceased child or grandchild to take the share of their deceased parent in equal parts among them: And where there shall be no children or descendants, then in equal parts to the next of kin in equal degree; and among collaterals, the children of a deceased brother or sister of the intestate shall have, in equal parts among them, their deceased parents' share; and there shall in no case be a distinction between kindred of the whole and half-blood; saving, in all cases, to the widow of the intestate her third part of the real estate for life, and one third part of the personal estate; and this law relative to descents and dower, shall remain in full force until altered by the legislature of the district. And until the governor and judges shall adopt laws as hereinafter mentioned, estates in the said territory may be devised or bequeathed by wills in writing, signed and sealed by him or her in whom the estate may be (being of full age), and attested by three witnesses; and real estates may be conveyed by lease and release, or bargain and sale, signed, sealed and delivered by the person being of full age, in whom the estate may be, and attested by two witnesses, provided such wills be duly proved, and such conveyances be acknowledged, or the execution thereof duly proved, and be recorded within one year after proper magistrates, courts, and registers shall be appointed for that purpose; and personal property may be transferred by delivery; saving, however to the French and Canadian inhabitants, and other settlers of the Kaskaskies, St. Vincents and the neighboring villages who have heretofore professed themselves citizens of Virginia, their laws and customs now in force among them, relative to the descent and conveyance, of property.

Section 3. Be it ordained by the authority aforesaid, That there shall be appointed from time to time by Congress, a governor, whose commission shall continue in force for the term of three years, unless sooner revoked by Congress; he shall reside in the district, and have a freehold estate therein in 1,000 acres of land, while in the exercise of his office.

Section 4. There shall be appointed from time to time by Congress, a secretary, whose commission shall continue in force for four years unless sooner revoked; he shall reside in the district, and have a freehold estate therein in 500 acres of land, while in the exercise of his office. It shall be his duty to keep and preserve the acts and laws passed by the legislature, and the public records of the district, and the proceedings of the governor in his executive department, and transmit authentic copies of such acts and proceedings, every six months, to the Secretary of Congress: There shall also be appointed a court to consist of three judges, any two of whom to form a court, who shall have a common law jurisdiction, and reside in the district, and have each therein a freehold estate in 500 acres of land while in the exercise of their offices; and their commissions shall continue in force during good behavior.

Section 5. The governor and judges, or a majority of them, shall adopt and publish in the district such laws of the original States, criminal and civil, as may be necessary and best suited to the circumstances of the district, and report them to Congress from time to time: which laws shall be in force in the district until the organization of the General Assembly therein, unless disapproved of by Congress; but afterwards the Legislature shall have authority to alter them as they shall think fit.

Section 6. The governor, for the time being, shall be commander in chief of the militia, appoint and commission all officers in the same below the rank of general officers; all general officers shall be appointed and commissioned by Congress.

Section 7. Previous to the organization of the general assembly, the governor shall appoint such magistrates and other civil officers in each county or township, as he shall find necessary for the preservation of the peace and good order in the same: After the general assembly shall be organized, the powers and duties of the magistrates and other civil officers shall be regulated and defined by the said assembly; but all magistrates and other civil officers not herein otherwise directed, shall during the continuance of this temporary government, be appointed by the governor.

Section 8. For the prevention of crimes and injuries, the laws to be adopted or made shall have force in all parts of the district, and for the execution of process, criminal and civil, the governor shall make proper divisions thereof; and he shall proceed from time to time as circumstances may require, to lay out the parts of the district in which the Indian titles shall have been extinguished, into counties and townships, subject, however, to such alterations as may thereafter be made by the legislature.

Section 9. So soon as there shall be five thousand free male inhabitants of full age in the district, upon giving proof thereof to the governor, they shall receive authority, with time and place, to elect a representative from their counties or townships to represent them in the general assembly: Provided, That, for every five hundred free male inhabitants, there shall be one representative, and so on progressively with the number of free male inhabitants shall the right of representation increase, until the number of representatives shall amount to twenty five; after which, the number and proportion of representatives shall be regulated by the legislature: Provided, That no person be eligible or qualified to act as a representative unless he shall have been a citizen of one of the United States three years, and be a resident in the district, or unless he shall have resided in the district three years; and, in either case, shall likewise hold in his own right, in fee simple, two hundred acres of land within the same; Provided, also, That a freehold in fifty acres of land in the district, having been a citizen of one of the states, and being resident in the district, or the like freehold and two years residence in the district, shall be necessary to qualify a man as an elector of a representative.

Section 10. The representatives thus elected, shall serve for the term of two years; and, in case of the death of a representative, or removal from office, the governor shall issue a writ to the county or township for which he was a member, to elect another in his stead, to serve for the residue of the term.

Section 11. The general assembly or legislature shall consist of the governor, legislative council, and a house of representatives. The Legislative Council shall consist of five members, to continue in office five years, unless sooner removed by Congress; any three of whom to be a quorum: and the members of the Council shall be nominated and appointed in the following manner, to wit: As soon as representatives shall be elected, the Governor shall appoint a time and place for them to meet together; and, when met, they shall nominate ten persons, residents in the district, and each possessed of a freehold in five hundred acres of land, and return their names to Congress;

five of whom Congress shall appoint and commission to serve as aforesaid; and, whenever a vacancy shall happen in the council, by death or removal from office, the house of representatives shall nominate two persons, qualified as aforesaid, for each vacancy, and return their names to Congress; one of whom congress shall appoint and commission for the residue of the term. And every five years, four months at least before the expiration of the time of service of the members of council, the said house shall nominate ten persons, qualified as aforesaid, and return their names to Congress; five of whom Congress shall appoint and commission to serve as members of the council five years, unless sooner removed. And the governor, legislative council, and house of representatives, shall have authority to make laws in all cases, for the good government of the district, not repugnant to the principles and articles in this ordinance established and declared. And all bills, having passed by a majority in the house, and by a majority in the council, shall be referred to the governor for his assent; but no bill, or legislative act whatever, shall be of any force without his assent. The governor shall have power to convene, prorogue, and dissolve the general assembly, when, in his opinion, it shall be expedient.

Section 12. The governor, judges, legislative council, secretary, and such other officers as Congress shall appoint in the district, shall take an oath or affirmation of fidelity and of office; the governor before the president of congress, and all other officers before the Governor. As soon as a legislature shall be formed in the district, the council and house assembled in one room, shall have authority, by joint ballot, to elect a delegate to Congress, who shall have a seat in Congress, with a right of debating but not voting during this temporary government.

Section 13. And, for extending the fundamental principles of civil and religious liberty, which form the basis whereon these republics, their laws and constitutions are erected; to fix and establish those principles as the basis of all laws, constitutions, and governments, which forever hereafter shall be formed in the said territory: to provide also for the establishment of States, and permanent government therein, and for their admission to a share in the federal councils on an equal footing with the original States, at as early periods as may be consistent with the general interest.

Section 14. It is hereby ordained and declared by the authority aforesaid, That the following articles shall be considered as articles of compact between the original States and the people and States in the said territory and forever remain unalterable, unless by common consent, to wit:

Article 1. No person, demeaning himself in a peaceable and orderly manner, shall ever be molested on account of his mode of worship or religious sentiments, in the said territory.

Article 2. The inhabitants of the said territory shall always be entitled to the benefits of the writ of habeas corpus, and of the trial by jury; of a proportionate representation of the people in the legislature; and of judicial proceedings according to the course of the common law. All persons shall be bailable, unless for capital offenses, where the proof shall be evident or the presumption great. All fines shall be moderate; and no cruel or unusual punishments shall be inflicted. No man shall be deprived of his liberty or property, but by the judgment of his peers or the law of the land; and, should the public exigencies make it necessary, for the common preservation, to take any person's property, or to demand his particular services, full compensation shall be made for the same. And, in the just preservation of rights and property, it is understood and declared, that no law ought ever to be made, or have force in the said territory, that shall, in any manner whatever, interfere with or affect private contracts or engagements, bona fide, and without fraud, previously formed.

Article 3. Religion, morality, and knowledge, being necessary to good government and the happiness of mankind, schools and the means of education shall forever be encouraged. The utmost good faith shall always be observed towards the Indians; their lands and property shall never be taken from them without their consent; and, in their property, rights, and liberty, they shall never be invaded or disturbed, unless in just and lawful wars authorized by Congress; but laws founded in justice and humanity, shall from time to time be made for preventing wrongs being done to them, and for preserving peace and friendship with them.

Article 4. The said territory, and the States which may be formed therein, shall forever remain a part of this Confederacy of the United States of America, subject to the Articles of Confederation, and to such alterations therein as shall be constitutionally made; and to all the acts and ordinances of the United States in Congress assembled, conformable thereto. The inhabitants and settlers in the said territory shall be subject to pay a part of the federal debts contracted or to be contracted, and a proportional part of the expenses of government, to be apportioned on them by Congress according to the same common rule and measure by which apportionments thereof shall be made on the other States; and the taxes for paying their proportion shall be laid and levied by the authority and direction of the legislatures of the district or districts, or new States, as in the original States, within the time agreed upon by the United States in Congress assembled. The legislatures of those districts or new States, shall never interfere with the primary disposal of the soil by the United States in Congress assembled, nor with any regulations Congress may find necessary for securing the title in such soil to the bona fide purchasers. No tax shall be imposed on lands the property of the United States; and, in no case, shall nonresident proprietors be taxed higher than residents. The navigable waters leading into the Mississippi and St. Lawrence, and the carrying places between the same, shall be common highways and forever free, as well to the inhabitants of the said territory as to the citizens of the United States, and those of any other States that may be admitted into the confederacy, without any tax, impost, or duty therefore.

Article 5. There shall be formed in the said territory, not less than three nor more than five States; and the boundaries of the States, as soon as Virginia shall alter her act of cession, and consent to the same, shall become fixed and established as follows, to wit: The western State in the said territory, shall be bounded by the Mississippi, the Ohio, and Wabash Rivers; a direct line drawn from the Wabash and Post Vincents, due North, to the territorial line between the United States and Canada; and, by the said territorial line, to the Lake of the Woods and Mississippi.

The middle State shall be bounded by the said direct line, the Wabash from Post Vincents to the Ohio, by the Ohio, by a direct line, drawn due north from the mouth of the Great Miami, to the said territorial line, and by the said territorial line. The eastern State shall be bounded by the last mentioned direct line, the Ohio, Pennsylvania, and the said territorial line: Provided, however, and it is further understood and declared, that the boundaries of these three States shall be subject so far to be altered, that, if Congress shall hereafter find it expedient, they shall have authority to form one or two States in that part of the said territory which lies north of an east and west line drawn through the southerly bend or extreme of Lake Michigan. And, whenever any of the said States shall have sixty thousand free inhabitants therein, such State shall be admitted, by its delegates, into the Congress of the United States, on an equal footing with the original States in all respects whatever, and shall be at liberty to form a permanent constitution and State government: Provided, the constitution and government so to be formed, shall be republican, and in conformity to the principles contained in these articles; and, so far as it can be consistent with the general interest of the confederacy, such admission shall be allowed at an earlier period, and when there may be a less number of free inhabitants in the State than sixty thousand.

Article 6. There shall be neither slavery nor involuntary servitude in the said territory, otherwise than in the punishment of crimes whereof the party shall have been duly convicted: Provided, always, That any person escaping into the same, from whom labor or service is lawfully claimed in any one of the original States, such fugitive may be lawfully reclaimed and conveyed to the person claiming his or her labor or service as aforesaid.

Be it ordained by the authority aforesaid, That the resolutions of the 23rd of April, 1784, relative to the subject of this ordinance, be, and the same are hereby repealed and declared null and void.

Done by the United States, in Congress assembled, the 13th day of July, in the year of our Lord 1787, and of their sovereignty and independence the twelfth.

Source: Government Printing Office, 1927. Selected and Indexed by Charles Tansill.

Lesson 7

Constitutional Convention of 1787

Without an alteration in our political creed, the superstructure we have been seven years in raising, at the expense of so much treasure and blood, must fall. We are fast verging to anarchy and confusion. Thirteen sovereignties pulling against each other, and all tugging at the Federal head, will soon bring ruin on the whole; whereas a liberal and energetic constitution, well checked and well watched to prevent encroachments, might restore us to that degree of respectability and consequence to which we had the fairest chance of attaining.

George Washington, Letter to James Madison, November 5, 1786

Compelling Question: What is the purpose of the United States Constitution?

Key Concepts

The delegates vigorously debated many issues at the Constitutional Convention. They had to compromise because the large and small states and the northern and southern states had different interests and goals. The most important compromises were about the new form of government and how to deal with the issue of slavery.

1. The delegates settled on a republican form of government with three equal branches: legislative, executive, and judicial. They also agreed on the Connecticut Compromise, which established a bicameral legislature. States would be represented equally in the Senate and by population in the House of Representatives.

2. Most of the delegates realized that slavery did not live up to the ideals of equality and liberty in the Declaration of Independence and that slavery would one day be abolished. But they also realized that they had to compromise with the southern states in order to create a union of all the states.

Need for a Constitutional Convention

After the thirteen original states won the war for independence from Britain, many of the shortcomings of the Articles of Confederation needed to be addressed. The Articles of Confederation had created a weak federal government—one too weak to fulfill its own duties. It had allowed the states to be sovereign, yet it unified them as a "confederation of perpetual union." Its Congress was the only governing body—there was no federal executive or judicial branch. Under the Articles of Confederation, Congress had the power to declare war, borrow money, create mail services, and regulate currency. But it could not enforce any of its laws by itself. It had to ask the states to both collect taxes to cover national expenses and enforce its laws.

To fix these shortcomings, the states called for a constitutional convention. The Constitutional Convention took place in Philadelphia from May 25 through September 17, 1787. Originally, the convention was meant to reform the Articles of Confederation. But instead, it proposed an entirely new constitution.

Delegates

States sent some of their best citizens to the Constitutional Convention. Among those attending were the Founders and leading thinkers James Madison, Alexander Hamilton, Gouverneur Morris, and Benjamin Franklin and war heroes Roger Sherman and John Dickinson.

Delegates were present from each state—except Rhode Island, whose delegates thought that any change to the Articles of Confederation would threaten states' sovereignty and, thus, their interests in trade. The Founders Samuel Adams and Patrick Henry chose not to attend because they disagreed with the principle of a strong national government. Thomas Jefferson, John Jay, and John Adams could not attend. John Jay was in New York serving as the Secretary of Foreign Affairs, and Adams and Jefferson were representing the country overseas at the time.

The delegates unanimously elected George Washington to preside over the convention. They agreed upon three rules for the proceedings of the convention: (1) that each state would have one vote, (2) that all present would maintain proper courtesy and order, and (3) that the proceedings of the convention would be kept secret.

Major Debates

The major points of contention in the Constitutional Convention were over how the federal government should be structured; how it could best represent the citizens and the states (see "The Plans"); and how to deal with the slavery issue.

Federalist versus Anti-Federalist debate. The Federalists believed that the federal government was too weak under the Articles of Confederation. They saw the need for a strong national government (including national defense). Alexander Hamilton, James Madison, and John Jay, writing under the name Publius, argued their case in a series of 85 newspaper articles titled *The Federalist Papers* (commonly called *"The Federalist"*). They provide great insight concerning the thinking and decisions made about the Constitution.

The Anti-Federalists argued against the expansion of national power beyond what was provided in the Articles of Confederation. They feared that centralized power would diminish individual rights and liberties.

Both sides came together to support the Bill of Rights before ratifying the U.S. Constitution.

The Plans. Two plans for restructuring the federal government were presented and debated at the Convention: the Virginia Plan and William Paterson's New Jersey Plan. Edmund Randolph presented the Virginia delegation's 15 resolutions, which replaced rather than reformed the Articles of Confederation. Madison was largely responsible for composing the plan. It proposed a government made up of three branches—executive, legislative, and judicial. The legislative branch would have two houses in which the states would be represented in proportion to their population, allowing larger states to have an advantage. Many members of smaller states sided with the New Jersey Plan, which proposed a reform of the Articles of Confederation that kept equal representation of the states regardless of their population size.

The delegates accepted the Connecticut Compromise, also called the "Great Compromise," proposed by Roger Sherman. The compromise presented a bicameral system that incorporated both methods of representation. In the House of Representatives, states would be represented based on population. In the Senate (as in the New Jersey Plan), each state would have equal representation regardless of population size.

Compromise on Slavery. Slavery forced the Founders to make difficult compromises. Most of the Founders realized that slavery was wrong and that it should be eliminated. Many of their personal letters referred to slavery as "a necessary evil." However, the harsh reality was that the southern states would not join with the middle and northern states to form one country if slavery were banned from the beginning. It was essential that the thirteen states had joined together to win the war against Great Britain. Now they had to remain united and stay strong in case Great Britain were to try to regain control of its former colonies. So, the northern and middle states accepted the evil of slavery as a problem to be dealt with in the future.

The following compromises were ultimately approved. (1) The Constitution allowed slaves to be counted as three-fifths of a person for the apportionment of congressional representatives and taxes. Antislavery delegates supported this compromise as a way to prevent the "slave states" from having more representation in Congress. The result was that the slave states had a voting minority in Congress. (2) The slave trade could not be banned prior to 1808. (3) And slaves who escaped to another state had to be returned to their homes. Known as the "Fugitive Slave Clause," Article IV, Section 2, gave no constitutional power to the federal or state governments to enforce it. The antislavery delegates compromised with slaveholding delegates in a way that had no force of law. The clause was repealed by the 13th Amendment.

The Founders were careful not to mention the word *slave* in the Constitution. Instead, they used the term *Person held to Service or Labour in one State, under the Laws thereof* to emphasize that there was no inherent right for one man to own another but that the laws of some states allowed it. Also, the term *Person held to Service or Labour* reflected the refusal of Madison and those who drafted the Constitution to validate the idea that people could be considered as property.

While the Founders made necessary compromises to forge a new nation, they considered all men (and women) to be equal in their natural rights and dedicated a new national government based on that proposition. But the compromises could not solve the problem of slavery being incompatible with freedom. Tragically, it took a bloody civil war for slavery to be extinguished, followed by the adoption of constitutional amendments granting legal rights to former slaves and finally to women.

Drafting and Ratification of the U.S. Constitution

After much debate, the **U.S. Constitution** was drafted, revised, and ultimately ratified. By late July, the convention appointed a Committee of Detail to revise the Virginia Plan and draft a constitution. The committee was made up of John Rutledge (South Carolina), Edmund Randolph (Virginia), Nathaniel Gorham (Massachusetts), Oliver Ellsworth (Connecticut), and James Wilson (Pennsylvania). As the primary writer of the document, Gouverneur Morris was responsible for most of the literary language and style of the Constitution.

Of the 55 original delegates, only 41 were present at the end of the convention, and all but three of the 41 approved and signed the document. The delegates that chose not to sign were Edmund Randolph of Virginia, George Mason of Virginia, and Elbridge Gerry of Massachusetts.

Congress then sent the Constitution to be ratified by each state. The Constitution was ratified, not by state legislatures, but by conventions elected by the people of each state. This ensured that the new American government would be established not just by state governments but also by the actions of the people.

Delaware was the first state to ratify the Constitution on December 7, 1787, and Rhode Island was the final state to ratify on May 29, 1790. In the end, all states voted to ratify the Constitution. By the time the ninth state—New Hampshire—ratified the Constitution on June 21, 1788, Congress passed a resolution to begin operating under the Constitution and to set dates for elections.

A Constitutional Republic Based on Natural Law

The Framers of the Constitution gave us a constitutional republic based on the foundation of the Declaration of Independence, which acknowledges that the rights of citizens do *not* come from the government. Rather, we have "inalienable rights endowed by [our] Creator," and it is the duty of our government to protect those rights. As declared in the Declaration of Independence, our Founders recognized the principles of Natural Law.

The chief function of the U.S. Constitution is to limit the power of the state. To eliminate confusion about the principle of "inalienable rights" in the Declaration of Independence as foundational to the Constitution, the Founders added the Bill of Rights as the first ten amendments (Session 13). The restrictive language in the Bill of Rights was added to prevent the government from abusing citizens' rights. Under this legal system, the rights of those in the minority are protected from abuse by the majority. "The United States shall guarantee to every State in the Union a Republican Form of government." [U.S. Constitution, Article IV, Section 4.]

■ Key Terms

constitutional republic. A form of government, such as that of the United States, in which the executive and legislators are elected by the people to represent them and protect their private property rights and other rights of citizens. Elected officials must follow the rules of the nation's constitution, and their actions are subject to judicial review. (See *republic* in Key Terms in Session 1.)

convention. A large meeting, or conference, often with delegates who vote on political matters.

delegate. A representative to a convention.

U.S. Constitution. The Founding Document of the United States of America that is the supreme law of the land and establishes the basic principles and framework of the federal government. It was ratified in 1788 and has since been modified by 27 amendments, including the Bill of Rights (first ten amendments) and 17 later amendments.

Discussion Questions

1. What were the weaknesses in the Articles of Confederation?

   Under the Articles of Confederation, Congress had the power to declare war, borrow money, create mail services, and regulate currency, but it had to rely on the states to enforce its laws. The governing Congress could not enforce any requests to the states or levy taxes to cover national expenses. In addition, the deliberating body could not make quick enough decisions for foreign affairs, the executive branch was weak, and there was no independent judicial branch.

2. How did the Constitutional Convention respond to those weaknesses?

   The convention members debated and determined how to make a stronger centralized federal government that would have the necessary powers to carry out its duties.

3. Who was elected to preside over the Constitutional Convention?

   George Washington

4. Name the competing plans presented at the Constitutional Convention? What did each plan seek to accomplish?

   The Virginia Plan proposed replacing the government then under the Articles of Confederation. It offered 15 resolutions to establish a new government with three branches: legislative, executive, and judicial. The New Jersey Plan instead sought to keep the current government in which each state had one vote in a unicameral legislature. The most important plan was the Connecticut Compromise—also known as the "Great Compromise." It established a bicameral legislative system with the House of Representatives and Senate. The delegates adopted this provision.

5. Who were the main authors of the Virginia Plan, New Jersey Plan, and Connecticut Compromise?

   James Madison, William Paterson, and Roger Sherman

6. What American document resulted from the Constitutional Convention?

   The United States Constitution

7. Even though slavery was prohibited in the Northwest Territory in accordance with the Northwest Ordinance of 1787, why did the Founders not outlaw slavery in the U.S. Constitution?

   The Founders knew they must unite all the states—even those with slaves—to win and maintain victory over Great Britain. They chose unity over ending the evil of slavery at that critical time in history. They expected to deal with slavery in the future, just not then.

CONSTITUTION OF THE UNITED STATES OF AMERICA

Adopted by the Congress September 17, 1787
Ratified by the States June 21, 1788

PREAMBLE

We the People of the United States, in Order to form a more perfect Union, establish Justice, insure domestic Tranquility, provide for the common defence, promote the general Welfare, and secure the Blessings of Liberty to ourselves and our Posterity, do ordain and establish this Constitution for the United States of America.

ARTICLE I

Section 1

All legislative Powers herein granted shall be vested in a Congress of the United States, which shall consist of a Senate and House of Representatives.

Section 2

The House of Representatives shall be composed of Members chosen every second Year by the People of the several States, and the Electors in each State shall have the Qualifications requisite for Electors of the most numerous Branch of the State Legislature. No Person shall be a Representative who shall not have attained to the Age of twenty five Years, and been seven Years a Citizen of the United States, and who shall not, when elected, be an Inhabitant of that State in which he shall be chosen.

Representatives and direct Taxes shall be apportioned among the several States which may be included within this Union, according to their respective Numbers, which shall be determined by adding to the whole Number of free Persons, including those bound to Service for a Term of Years, and excluding Indians not taxed, three fifths of all other Persons. The actual Enumeration shall be made within three Years after the first Meeting of the Congress of the United States, and within every subsequent Term of ten Years, in such Manner as they shall by Law direct. The Number of Representatives shall not exceed one for every thirty Thousand, but each State shall have at Least one Representative; and until such enumeration shall be made, the State of New Hampshire shall be entitled to chuse three, Massachusetts eight, Rhode-Island and Providence Plantations one, Connecticut five, New-York six, New Jersey four, Pennsylvania eight, Delaware one, Maryland six, Virginia ten, North Carolina five, South Carolina five, and Georgia three.

When vacancies happen in the Representation from any State, the Executive Authority thereof shall issue Writs of Election to fill such Vacancies.

The House of Representatives shall chuse their Speaker and other Officers; and shall have the sole Power of Impeachment.

Section 3

The Senate of the United States shall be composed of two Senators from each State, chosen by the Legislature thereof, for six Years; and each Senator shall have one Vote.

Immediately after they shall be assembled in Consequence of the first Election, they shall be divided as equally as may be into three Classes. The Seats of the Senators of the first Class shall be vacated at the Expiration of the second Year, of the second Class at the Expiration of the fourth Year, and of the third Class at the Expiration of the sixth Year, so that one third may be chosen every second Year; and if Vacancies happen by Resignation, or otherwise, during the Recess of the Legislature of any State, the Executive thereof may make temporary Appointments until the next Meeting of the Legislature, which shall then fill such Vacancies.

No Person shall be a Senator who shall not have attained to the Age of thirty Years, and been nine Years a Citizen of the United States, and who shall not, when elected, be an Inhabitant of that State for which he shall be chosen.

The Vice President of the United States shall be President of the Senate, but shall have no Vote, unless they be equally divided.

The Senate shall chuse their other Officers, and also a President pro tempore, in the Absence of the Vice President, or when he shall exercise the Office of President of the United States.

The Senate shall have the sole Power to try all Impeachments. When sitting for that Purpose, they shall be on Oath or Affirmation. When the President of the United States is tried, the Chief Justice shall preside: And no Person shall be convicted without the Concurrence of two thirds of the Members present.

Judgment in Cases of Impeachment shall not extend further than to removal from Office, and disqualification to hold and enjoy any Office of honor, Trust or Profit under the United States: but the Party convicted shall nevertheless be liable and subject to Indictment, Trial, Judgment and Punishment, according to Law.

Section 4

The Times, Places and Manner of holding Elections for Senators and Representatives, shall be prescribed in each State by the Legislature thereof; but the Congress may at any time by Law make or alter such Regulations, except as to the Places of chusing Senators.

The Congress shall assemble at least once in every Year, and such Meeting shall be on the first Monday in December, unless they shall by Law appoint a different Day.

Section 5

Each House shall be the Judge of the Elections, Returns and Qualifications of its own Members, and a Majority of each shall constitute a Quorum to do Business; but a smaller Number may adjourn from day to day, and may be authorized to compel the Attendance of absent Members, in such Manner, and under such Penalties as each House may provide.

Each House may determine the Rules of its Proceedings, punish its Members for disorderly Behaviour, and, with the Concurrence of two thirds, expel a Member.

Each House shall keep a Journal of its Proceedings, and from time to time publish the same, excepting such Parts as may in their Judgment require Secrecy; and the Yeas and Nays of the

Members of either House on any question shall, at the Desire of one fifth of those Present, be entered on the Journal.

Neither House, during the Session of Congress, shall, without the Consent of the other, adjourn for more than three days, nor to any other Place than that in which the two Houses shall be sitting.

Section 6

The Senators and Representatives shall receive a Compensation for their Services, to be ascertained by Law, and paid out of the Treasury of the United States. They shall in all Cases, except Treason, Felony and Breach of the Peace, be privileged from Arrest during their Attendance at the Session of their respective Houses, and in going to and returning from the same; and for any Speech or Debate in either House, they shall not be questioned in any other Place.

No Senator or Representative shall, during the Time for which he was elected, be appointed to any civil Office under the Authority of the United States, which shall have been created, or the Emoluments whereof shall have been encreased during such time; and no Person holding any Office under the United States, shall be a Member of either House during his Continuance in Office.

Section 7

All Bills for raising Revenue shall originate in the House of Representatives; but the Senate may propose or concur with Amendments as on other Bills.

Every Bill which shall have passed the House of Representatives and the Senate, shall, before it become a Law, be presented to the President of the United States: If he approve he shall sign it, but if not he shall return it, with his Objections to that House in which it shall have originated, who shall enter the Objections at large on their Journal, and proceed to reconsider it. If after such Reconsideration two thirds of that House shall agree to pass the Bill, it shall be sent, together with the Objections, to the other House, by which it shall likewise be reconsidered, and if approved by two thirds of that House, it shall become a Law. But in all such Cases the Votes of both Houses shall be determined by Yeas and Nays, and the Names of the Persons voting for and against the Bill shall be entered on the Journal of each House respectively. If any Bill shall not be returned by the President within ten Days (Sundays excepted) after it shall have been presented to him, the Same shall be a Law, in like Manner as if he had signed it, unless the Congress by their Adjournment prevent its Return, in which Case it shall not be a Law.

Every Order, Resolution, or Vote to which the Concurrence of the Senate and House of Representatives may be necessary (except on a question of Adjournment) shall be presented to the President of the United States; and before the Same shall take Effect, shall be approved by him, or being disapproved by him, shall be re-passed by two thirds of the Senate and House of Representatives, according to the Rules and Limitations prescribed in the Case of a Bill.

Section 8

The Congress shall have Power To lay and collect Taxes, Duties, Imposts and Excises, to pay the Debts and provide for the common Defence and general Welfare of the United States; but all Duties, Imposts and Excises shall be uniform throughout the United States;

To borrow Money on the credit of the United States;

To regulate Commerce with foreign Nations, and among the several States, and with the Indian Tribes;

To establish an uniform Rule of Naturalization, and uniform Laws on the subject of Bankruptcies throughout the United States;

To coin Money, regulate the Value thereof, and of foreign Coin, and fix the Standard of Weights and Measures;

To provide for the Punishment of counterfeiting the Securities and current Coin of the United States;

To establish Post Offices and post Roads;

To promote the Progress of Science and useful Arts, by securing for limited Times to Authors and Inventors the exclusive Right to their respective Writings and Discoveries;

To constitute Tribunals inferior to the supreme Court;

To define and punish Piracies and Felonies committed on the high Seas, and Offences against the Law of Nations;

To declare War, grant Letters of Marque and Reprisal, and make Rules concerning Captures on Land and Water;

To raise and support Armies, but no Appropriation of Money to that Use shall be for a longer Term than two Years;

To provide and maintain a Navy;

To make Rules for the Government and Regulation of the land and naval Forces;

To provide for calling forth the Militia to execute the Laws of the Union, suppress Insurrections and repel Invasions;

To provide for organizing, arming, and disciplining, the Militia, and for governing such Part of them as may be employed in the Service of the United States, reserving to the States respectively, the Appointment of the Officers, and the Authority of training the Militia according to the discipline prescribed by Congress;

To exercise exclusive Legislation in all Cases whatsoever, over such District (not exceeding ten Miles square) as may, by Cession of particular States, and the Acceptance of Congress, become the Seat of the Government of the United States, and to exercise like Authority over all Places purchased by the Consent of the Legislature of the State in which the Same shall be, for the Erection of Forts, Magazines, Arsenals, dock-Yards, and other needful Buildings;—And

To make all Laws which shall be necessary and proper for carrying into Execution the foregoing Powers, and all other Powers vested by this Constitution in the Government of the United States, or in any Department or Officer thereof.

Section 9

The Migration or Importation of such Persons as any of the States now existing shall think proper to admit, shall not be prohibited by the Congress prior to the Year one thousand eight hundred and eight, but a Tax or duty may be imposed on such Importation, not exceeding ten dollars for each Person.

The Privilege of the Writ of Habeas Corpus shall not be suspended, unless when in Cases of Rebellion or Invasion the public Safety may require it.

No Bill of Attainder or ex post facto Law shall be passed.

No Capitation, or other direct, Tax shall be laid, unless in Proportion to the Census or enumeration herein before directed to be taken.

No Tax or Duty shall be laid on Articles exported from any State.

No Preference shall be given by any Regulation of Commerce or Revenue to the Ports of one State over those of another; nor shall Vessels bound to, or from, one State, be obliged to enter, clear, or pay Duties in another.

No Money shall be drawn from the Treasury, but in Consequence of Appropriations made by Law; and a regular Statement and Account of the Receipts and Expenditures of all public Money shall be published from time to time.

No Title of Nobility shall be granted by the United States: And no Person holding any Office of Profit or Trust under them, shall, without the Consent of the Congress, accept of any present, Emolument, Office, or Title, of any kind whatever, from any King, Prince, or foreign State.

Section 10

No State shall enter into any Treaty, Alliance, or Confederation; grant Letters of Marque and Reprisal; coin Money; emit Bills of Credit; make any Thing but gold and silver Coin a Tender in Payment of Debts; pass any Bill of Attainder, ex post facto Law, or Law impairing the Obligation of Contracts, or grant any Title of Nobility.

No State shall, without the Consent of the Congress, lay any Imposts or Duties on Imports or Exports, except what may be absolutely necessary for executing its inspection Laws: and the net Produce of all Duties and Imposts, laid by any State on Imports or Exports, shall be for the Use of the Treasury of the United States; and all such Laws shall be subject to the Revision and Control of the Congress.

No State shall, without the Consent of Congress, lay any Duty of Tonnage, keep Troops, or Ships of War in time of Peace, enter into any Agreement or Compact with another State, or with a foreign Power, or engage in War, unless actually invaded, or in such imminent Danger as will not admit of delay.

ARTICLE II

Section 1

The executive Power shall be vested in a President of the United States of America. He shall hold his Office during the Term of four Years, and, together with the Vice-President, chosen for the same Term, be elected, as follows:

Each State shall appoint, in such Manner as the Legislature thereof may direct, a Number of Electors, equal to the whole Number of Senators and Representatives to which the State may be entitled in the Congress: but no Senator or Representative, or Person holding an Office of Trust or Profit under the United States, shall be appointed an Elector.

The Electors shall meet in their respective States, and vote by Ballot for two Persons, of whom one at least shall not be an Inhabitant of the same State with themselves. And they shall make a List of all the Persons voted for, and of the Number of Votes for each; which List they shall sign and certify, and transmit sealed to the Seat of the Government of the United States, directed to the

President of the Senate. The President of the Senate shall, in the Presence of the Senate and House of Representatives, open all the Certificates, and the Votes shall then be counted. The Person having the greatest Number of Votes shall be the President, if such Number be a Majority of the whole Number of Electors appointed; and if there be more than one who have such Majority, and have an equal Number of Votes, then the House of Representatives shall immediately chuse by Ballot one of them for President; and if no Person have a Majority, then from the five highest on the List the said House shall in like Manner chuse the President. But in chusing the President, the Votes shall be taken by States, the Representatives from each State having one Vote; a quorum for this Purpose shall consist of a Member or Members from two thirds of the States, and a Majority of all the States shall be necessary to a Choice. In every Case, after the Choice of the President, the Person having the greatest Number of Votes of the Electors shall be the Vice President. But if there should remain two or more who have equal Votes, the Senate shall chuse from them by Ballot the Vice President.

The Congress may determine the Time of chusing the Electors, and the Day on which they shall give their Votes; which Day shall be the same throughout the United States.

No Person except a natural born Citizen, or a Citizen of the United States, at the time of the Adoption of this Constitution, shall be eligible to the Office of President; neither shall any person be eligible to that Office who shall not have attained to the Age of thirty five Years, and been fourteen Years a Resident within the United States.

In Case of the Removal of the President from Office, or of his Death, Resignation, or Inability to discharge the Powers and Duties of the said Office, the Same shall devolve on the Vice President, and the Congress may by Law provide for the Case of Removal, Death, Resignation or Inability, both of the President and Vice President, declaring what Officer shall then act as President, and such Officer shall act accordingly, until the Disability be removed, or a President shall be elected.

The President shall, at stated Times, receive for his Services, a Compensation, which shall neither be increased nor diminished during the Period for which he shall have been elected, and he shall not receive within that Period any other Emolument from the United States, or any of them.

Before he enter on the Execution of his Office, he shall take the following Oath or Affirmation: "I do solemnly swear (or affirm) that I will faithfully execute the Office of President of the United States, and will to the best of my Ability, preserve, protect and defend the Constitution of the United States."

Section 2

The President shall be Commander in Chief of the Army and Navy of the United States, and of the Militia of the several States, when called into the actual Service of the United States; he may require the Opinion, in writing, of the principal Officer in each of the executive Departments, upon any Subject relating to the Duties of their respective Offices, and he shall have Power to Grant Reprieves and Pardons for Offences against the United States, except in Cases of Impeachment.

He shall have Power, by and with the Advice and Consent of the Senate, to make Treaties, provided two thirds of the Senators present concur; and he shall nominate, and by and with the Advice and Consent of the Senate, shall appoint Ambassadors, other public Ministers and Consuls, Judges of the supreme Court, and all other Officers of the United States, whose Appointments are not herein otherwise provided for, and which shall be established by Law: but the Congress may by Law vest the Appointment of such inferior Officers, as they think proper, in the President alone, in the Courts of Law, or in the Heads of Departments.

The President shall have Power to fill up all Vacancies that may happen during the Recess of the Senate, by granting Commissions which shall expire at the End of their next Session.

Section 3

He shall from time to time give to the Congress Information on the State of the Union, and recommend to their Consideration such Measures as he shall judge necessary and expedient; he may, on extraordinary Occasions, convene both Houses, or either of them, and in Case of Disagreement between them, with Respect to the Time of Adjournment, he may adjourn them to such Time as he shall think proper; he shall receive Ambassadors and other public Ministers; he shall take Care that the Laws be faithfully executed, and shall Commission all the Officers of the United States.

Section 4

The President, Vice President and all Civil Officers of the United States, shall be removed from Office on Impeachment for, and Conviction of, Treason, Bribery, or other high Crimes and Misdemeanors.

ARTICLE III

Section 1

The judicial Power of the United States, shall be vested in one supreme Court, and in such inferior Courts as the Congress may from time to time ordain and establish. The Judges, both of the supreme and inferior Courts, shall hold their Offices during good Behaviour, and shall, at stated Times, receive for their Services, a Compensation, which shall not be diminished during their Continuance in Office.

Section 2

The judicial Power shall extend to all Cases, in Law and Equity, arising under this Constitution, the Laws of the United States, and Treaties made, or which shall be made, under their Authority;—to all Cases affecting Ambassadors, other public ministers and Consuls;—to all Cases of admiralty and maritime Jurisdiction;—to Controversies to which the United States shall be a Party;—to Controversies between two or more States;—between a State and Citizens of another State;—between Citizens of different States;—between Citizens of the same State claiming Lands under Grants of different States, and between a State, or the Citizens thereof, and foreign States, Citizens or Subjects.

In all Cases affecting Ambassadors, other public Ministers and Consuls, and those in which a State shall be Party, the supreme Court shall have original Jurisdiction. In all the other Cases before mentioned, the supreme Court shall have appellate Jurisdiction, both as to Law and Fact, with such Exceptions, and under such Regulations as the Congress shall make.

The Trial of all Crimes, except in Cases of Impeachment, shall be by Jury; and such Trial shall be held in the State where the said Crimes shall have been committed; but when not committed within any State, the Trial shall be at such Place or Places as the Congress may by Law have directed.

Section 3

Treason against the United States, shall consist only in levying War against them, or in adhering to their Enemies, giving them Aid and Comfort. No Person shall be convicted of Treason unless on the Testimony of two Witnesses to the same overt Act, or on Confession in open Court.

The Congress shall have Power to declare the Punishment of Treason, but no Attainder of Treason shall work Corruption of Blood, or Forfeiture except during the Life of the Person attainted.

ARTICLE IV

Section 1

Full Faith and Credit shall be given in each State to the public Acts, Records, and judicial Proceedings of every other State. And the Congress may by general Laws prescribe the Manner in which such Acts, Records and Proceedings shall be proved, and the Effect thereof.

Section 2

The Citizens of each State shall be entitled to all Privileges and Immunities of Citizens in the several States.

A Person charged in any State with Treason, Felony, or other Crime, who shall flee from Justice, and be found in another State, shall on Demand of the executive Authority of the State from which he fled, be delivered up, to be removed to the State having Jurisdiction of the Crime.

No Person held to Service or Labour in one State, under the Laws thereof, escaping into another, shall, in Consequence of any Law or Regulation therein, be discharged from such Service or Labour, but shall be delivered up on Claim of the Party to whom such Service or Labour may be due.

Section 3

New States may be admitted by the Congress into this Union; but no new State shall be formed or erected within the Jurisdiction of any other State; nor any State be formed by the Junction of two or more States, or Parts of States, without the Consent of the Legislatures of the States concerned as well as of the Congress.

The Congress shall have Power to dispose of and make all needful Rules and Regulations respecting the Territory or other Property belonging to the United States; and nothing in this Constitution shall be so construed as to Prejudice any Claims of the United States, or of any particular State.

Section 4

The United States shall guarantee to every State in this Union a Republican Form of Government, and shall protect each of them against Invasion; and on Application of the Legislature, or of the Executive (when the Legislature cannot be convened) against domestic Violence.

ARTICLE V

The Congress, whenever two thirds of both Houses shall deem it necessary, shall propose Amendments to this Constitution, or, on the Application of the Legislatures of two thirds of the several States, shall call a Convention for proposing Amendments, which, in either Case, shall be valid to all Intents and Purposes, as Part of this Constitution, when ratified by the Legislatures of three fourths of the several States, or by Conventions in three fourths thereof, as the one or the other Mode of Ratification may be proposed by the Congress; Provided that no Amendment which may be made prior to the Year One thousand eight hundred and eight shall in any Manner affect the first and fourth Clauses in the Ninth Section of the first Article; and that no State, without its Consent, shall be deprived of its equal Suffrage in the Senate.

ARTICLE VI

All Debts contracted and Engagements entered into, before the Adoption of this Constitution, shall be as valid against the United States under this Constitution, as under the Confederation.

This Constitution, and the Laws of the United States which shall be made in Pursuance thereof; and all Treaties made, or which shall be made, under the Authority of the United States, shall be the supreme Law of the Land; and the Judges in every State shall be bound thereby, any Thing in the Constitution or Laws of any State to the Contrary notwithstanding.

The Senators and Representatives before mentioned, and the Members of the several State Legislatures, and all executive and judicial Officers, both of the United States and of the several States, shall be bound by Oath or Affirmation, to support this Constitution; but no religious Test shall ever be required as a Qualification to any Office or public Trust under the United States.

ARTICLE VII

The Ratification of the Conventions of nine States, shall be sufficient for the Establishment of this Constitution between the States so ratifying the Same.

DONE in Convention by the Unanimous Consent of the States present the Seventeenth Day of September in the Year of our Lord one thousand seven hundred and Eighty-seven and of the Independence of the United States of America the Twelfth.

In WITNESS whereof We have hereunto subscribed our Names,

George Washington: President and deputy from Virginia

New Hampshire: John Langdon, Nicholas Gilman

Massachusetts: Nathaniel Gorham, Rufus King

Connecticut: William Samuel Johnson, Roger Sherman

New York: Alexander Hamilton

New Jersey: William Livingston, David Brearley, William Paterson, Jonathan Dayton

Pennsylvania: Benjamin Franklin, Robert Morris, Thomas Fitzsimons, James Wilson, Thomas Mifflin, George Clymer, Jared Ingersoll, Gouverneur Morris

Delaware: George Read, John Dickinson, Jacob Broom, Gunning Bedford, Jr., Richard Bassett

Maryland: James McHenry, Daniel Carroll, Daniel of St. Thomas Jenifer

Virginia: John Blair, James Madison, Jr.

North Carolina: William Blount, Hugh Williamson, Richard Dobbs Spaight

South Carolina: John Rutledge, Charles Pinckney, Charles Cotesworth Pinckney, Pierce Butler

Georgia: William Few, Abraham Baldwin

Attesting: William Jackson, Secretary

Lesson 8

U.S. Constitution Preamble and Article I. Legislative Branch

The powers of the legislature are defined, and limited; and that those limits may not be mistaken, or forgotten, the Constitution is written.
Chief Justice John Marshall, Marbury v. Madison, 1803

Compelling Question: How did the writers of the Constitution protect the United States from tyranny?

Key Concepts

1. The Preamble to the Constitution lists the Founders' reasons for forming a new federal government and lays out the purpose of the U.S. Constitution and the union it established.

2. The first article of the Constitution describes the Congress—the branch most representative of the people. It grants the legislative branch the power to make laws so the federal government can carry out the will of the people.

3. The legislative branch consists of the two houses of Congress: the Senate and the House of Representatives.

4. Congressional powers are specifically enumerated, and Congress has authority to effectively exercise those powers. Congress is the only body that has the power to propose and pass bills.

Preamble to the Constitution: Reasons for Forming the New Government

In contrast to the beginning of the Articles of Confederation, which emphasizes individual states, the Preamble to the Constitution declares that "We the People" are responsible for establishing this new government. The Constitution then lists six reasons for forming the new government: "to form a more perfect Union, establish Justice, insure domestic Tranquility, provide for the common defence, promote the general Welfare, and secure the Blessings of liberty to ourselves and our Posterity." (See "Modern Interpretation of 'Promote the General Welfare'" before Key Terms in this session.)

Purpose and Powers of the Branches of Government

The Founders carefully crafted the Constitution. They recognized that the people have inalienable rights and that the purpose of government is to preserve those rights. The Constitution does not give the federal government as a whole any rights or powers.

Instead, the Founders designed three branches of government that have specific limited powers (not rights) granted by the Constitution.

The Constitution consists of seven articles, which are divided into sections and clauses. The first three articles focus on the three branches of the federal government—legislative, executive, and judicial. The articles state the branches' unique, but limited, powers, functions, and responsibilities.

Each branch's powers are stated in a vesting clause found in Section 1 of the first three articles. By defining the scope of powers of each branch, these clauses create a separation of powers between the branches. The U.S. Congress is granted legislative power, the president is granted executive power, and the federal judiciary is granted judicial power.

Legislative Branch with Two Houses of Congress

Article I, Section 1's **Vesting Clause** specifically grants Congress all power to legislate.

Article I, Sections 2–7, describe the structure and function of the two houses of Congress. The legislative branch is the most democratic of the three branches because it is the one most directly controlled by the people of the United States. The Founders intended the House of Representatives to be more reflective of and responsive to public opinion. They intended the Senate to be more deliberative, with a long-term perspective on the concerns of the nation. Because of its deliberative nature, the Senate also performs the duties of approving international treaties and presidential appointments.

The Founders intent for each house (or chamber) is reflected in their minimum age requirements and length of terms. Senators must be at least 30 years old, and their terms are for six years. Representatives must be at least 25 years old, and their terms are for two years. Senators and representatives have no limit to the number of terms they can serve if reelected.

The process for passing bills is addressed in Section 7. The House of Representatives is said to have the **"power of the purse"** because all bills to raise revenue must originate in the House. All other bills may originate in either the House of Representatives or the Senate.

Each house may amend the bills. Both houses must pass the identical bill by a majority (more than 50 percent) before it goes to the president for his (or her) signature or veto. A bill doesn't become law until the president signs it or lets it pass without his (or her) signature after ten days. (The president's role in this process is discussed in Session 9, Executive Branch.)

Enumerated Legislative Powers

In Article I, Section 8, the Constitution describes the legislative branch's **enumerated powers**. Pay careful attention to the powers given to the legislative branch and how they secure the purposes of the federal government stated in the Preamble. When reading the powers, think about why these powers given to the legislative branch are best exercised by the federal government rather than by state governments. Keep the legislative powers in mind, especially as they relate to the powers of the other branches. The Constitution vests specific powers in each branch to provide **checks and balances** to the other branches, which each have specific duties.

All but two powers in Section 8 were part of the Articles of Confederation. The added powers were to correct weaknesses in the Articles of Confederation. In the Constitution, the Founders gave the legislative branch new powers to levy taxes and to regulate commerce internationally and among the states.

The Founders sought to create a federal government strong enough to act decisively. But they knew that legislative powers must be limited to those enumerated in the Constitution to avoid abuse of power. The Necessary and Proper Clause at the end of Section 8 allows Congress "[t]o make all laws which shall be necessary and proper" to execute the powers enumerated in Article I, Section 8. Congress was not to expand its powers at all. Powers not specifically granted to the federal government were reserved for the state governments. Even the Founders disagreed about interpretation of the Necessary and Proper Clause. Hamilton interpreted the clause loosely. Jefferson interpreted it strictly. Madison argued that the clause didn't give the federal government any additional powers.

Limits to Powers

Section 9 limits the powers of the legislative branch. Briefly, Congress has no power to suspend certain rights of citizens and is limited in how it levies taxes.

Section 10 limits the powers of the states. They cannot enter into treaties with other nations or coin their own money.

Both Congress and the states are prohibited from granting titles of nobility, such as duke or duchess, count or countess. The Founders feared that any titles of nobility would endanger the principle of equality found in the Declaration of Independence and the Constitution.

Also, no government official may accept any gifts or compensation from foreign governments.

Modern Interpretation of "Promote the General Welfare"

In the last 100 years, the interpretation of "promote the general welfare" in the Preamble has resulted in a broad expansion of the scope and power of the federal government beyond what the Founders referred to in the Constitution. Consider that the Founders would have been clear on the meaning of *general welfare* and that it was quite different from the current definition. "The Founders clearly understood the 'general welfare' to mean the good of all citizens, not an open-ended mandate for Congress. The only good that applies to all citizens is freedom, and government's proper role is the protection of that freedom. This was the meaning intended by the Founders." ("The Founders and the General Welfare," https:// individualrightsgovernmentwrongs.com/founding-fathers/the-founders-and-the-general- welfare)

The noted historian Dr. Clarence Carson (Foundation for Economic Education, 1983) writes: "What Americans began calling welfare programs in the late 1930s, or thereabouts, the Founders would have known by the name of 'poor relief,' so far as they were familiar with it at all. In England, tax supported relief of the poor [and those unable to work] was required under the 'poor laws,' more specifically, the Elizabethan Poor Law, during the American colonial period."

Dr. Carson goes on to say, "No one at the time of the writing of the Constitution would have associated the life of the poor dependent upon public relief with the word welfare. 'Welfare,' in common usage for centuries, stems from the roots 'well' and 'fare,' and means basically, according to my dictionary, a 'state of faring well; well-being.' Synonyms are: 'Prosperity, success, happiness, weal.' No sensible person would have confused poor relief with prosperity, success, or even faring well. Indeed, it was in every respect the opposite."

But the definition of promoting the general welfare has changed dramatically over the last century to include providing a safety net for citizens who are unemployed, disabled, and living in poverty. This has resulted in a change in the basic role of the federal government. Ratified in 1913, the 16th Amendment authorized a federal income tax, providing the means for Congress to tax individual citizens directly and take on immense levels of debt. (See Session 15.) The new definition of promoting the general welfare and the new source of tax dollars led to Congress passing legislation to provide federal aid for citizens deemed to be in need. Over the years, Congress passed many laws that forever changed the United States, including Social Security (1935), Medicare and Medicaid (1965), and other social welfare programs, sometimes referred to as "entitlement programs."

While these programs are well-meaning and have brought immediate relief to millions, we must count the cost to future generations. The federal debt stood at more than $28 trillion at the end of 2021. According to a recent forecast by the Congressional Budget Office, this debt is projected to rise to $31.4 trillion at the end of 2030—an amount equal to 98 percent of gross domestic product. That's the highest since the end of World War II!

Even more concerning is that this does not count the unfunded liabilities, such as Social Security and Medicare entitlements that the government is obligated to pay in the future, estimated to be more than $50 trillion! Most economists agree that this situation is not sustainable and must be addressed by Congress.

■ Key Terms

bill. The draft of a proposed law, which is presented, debated, and approved or rejected by the legislative branch. If approved, it is sent to the executive branch, where it may become law by action of the president.

checks and balances. The principle, or system, in the U.S. Constitution in which each separate branch of the government has some power to check (change or overturn) certain actions by the other two branches. The purpose is to provide balance among the branches and to ensure that political power is not concentrated in the hands of any individual or group so that no branch of government becomes too powerful.

enumerated powers. The list of powers that the Constitution specifically grants to Congress in Article I, Section 8.

house. Either chamber of Congress (the House of Representatives or the Senate). When capitalized, it usually refers to the House of Representatives.

Necessary and Proper Clause. The last clause in Article I, Section 8, of the Constitution, which grants Congress the power to make all laws necessary for executing its enumerated powers and all other powers of the federal government as a whole.

power of the purse. The power of the House of Representatives to initiate all bills for raising revenue.

preamble. An opening statement, or introduction, especially to the U.S. Constitution, which states the reasons for and intent of the document.

Vesting Clause. The clauses in Section 1 of Articles I, II, and III of the Constitution that give legislative power to the U.S. Congress, executive power to the U.S. president, and judicial power to the federal judiciary, respectively.

Discussion Questions

1. What is distinctive about the Preamble, and what did it establish for today?

   The Preamble begins with "We the people." The Preamble explains the purposes of the government. These purposes are still true of the United States government today as we live under the same Constitution.

2. What are the basic purposes of the United States government?

   From the Preamble to the Constitution: "to form a more perfect union, establish justice, ensure domestic tranquility, provide for the common defence, promote the general welfare, and to secure the blessings of liberty to ourselves and our posterity." From the Declaration of Independence: to secure the rights of "life, liberty, and the pursuit of happiness."

3. Why are these purposes better accomplished by the federal government than by the states? Give an example of why it is better for the federal government to have the power and decide on some things rather than the individual states.

   The Founders recognized that many things should be decided by the national government on behalf of all the states, such as establishing a national currency and going to war. They established federal powers vested in the legislative branch so the federal government could act with authority to unite the states under one limited government. Matters that were not the responsibility of the entire nation were left to the states.

4. What are the three branches of the federal government provided by the Constitution?

   Legislative, executive, and judicial

5. What did the Founders intend by designing a bicameral Congress composed of the House of Representatives and the Senate? How do these two houses accomplish the overall goals of the legislative branch?

   The Founders debated how best to represent both the voice of the people and the concerns of the states. They resolved the debate by creating a bicameral legislature, each house with different requirements for election, structure, and powers. The Constitution says that the House of Representatives shall have representatives from each state according to its population. The Senate shall have two senators, each with one vote, totaling two votes per state, regardless of its population. This balances the voice of the people and the states in legislative decisions.

6. Explain the Necessary and Proper Clause.

   The Necessary and Proper Clause prohibits Congress from expanding its powers at all. Rather, Congress shall adopt only the means necessary to carry out the powers enumerated in Article 1, Section 8. The legislative branch is authorized to adopt the means it needs to accomplish its specific duties, but only those which are necessary to act on the specific powers granted.

7. In what ways do the specific enumerated powers of Congress fulfill the requirements of constitutional government and answer the previous problems of the Articles of Confederation?

   Among the problems under the Articles of Confederation was that the individual states were all coequal within a single chamber of congress. Each state was in perpetual competition with the others. And there was no clearly defined chief executive, other than the president of the Congress, who had no defined authority to act. To remedy these flaws and to strengthen constitutional government, the Founders created a legislative structure in the Constitution that balances congressional power between states with large populations and each state as an equal member of the union. The Constitution creates an incentive for the houses of Congress to seek compromise. The incentive for states to seek compromise in the chambers of Congress is strengthened by the Constitution's enumerated powers.

   Each branch of the federal government has specific limited responsibilities to accomplish and specific limited authority to act. Furthermore, by establishing an executive branch separate from Congress, with its own responsibilities and authority, the Constitution fixed the shortfalls that had doomed the Articles of Confederation to failure.

8. How does Congress pass a bill? How does a bill become a law? Explain this process.

   See "How Does a Bill Become a Law?" that follows. All bills except those which raise revenue may be proposed by either house of Congress. Only the House of Representatives has the "power of the purse." Bills are often amended during the deliberation process. To become law, the same bill must pass both houses by a majority. Once the identical bill has passed both the House of Representatives and the Senate, it must be presented to the president, who can either sign it into law or veto it and return it to be reconsidered with his objections attached. The House and the Senate may override a veto by a two-thirds vote, and then the bill will become law. If after the first time he or she receives it, the president does not return it to the house of Congress that originated the bill within ten days, it will automatically become law.

HOW DOES A BILL BECOME A LAW?

1. EVERY LAW STARTS WITH AN IDEA

That idea can come from anyone, even you! Contact your elected officials to share your idea. If they want to try to make it a law, they will write a bill.

2. THE BILL IS INTRODUCED

A bill can start in either house of Congress when it's introduced by its primary sponsor, a Senator or a Representative. In the House of Representatives, bills are placed in a wooden box called "the hopper."

Here, the bill is assigned a legislative number before the Speaker of the House sends it to a committee.

3. THE BILL GOES TO COMMITTEE

Representatives or Senators meet in a small group to research, talk about, and make changes to the bill. They vote to accept or reject the bill and its changes before sending it to:

the House or Senate floor for debate or to a subcommittee for further research.

4. CONGRESS DEBATES AND VOTES

Members of the House or Senate can now debate the bill and propose changes or amendments before voting. If the majority vote for and pass the bill, it moves to the other house to go through a similar process of committees, debate, and voting. Both houses have to agree on the same version of the final bill before it goes to the President.

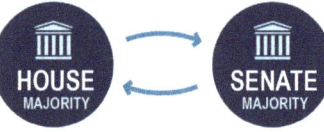

DID YOU KNOW?
The House uses an electronic voting system while the Senate typically votes by voice, saying "yay" or "nay."

5. PRESIDENTIAL ACTION

When the bill reaches the President, he or she can:

 **APPROVE and PASS**
The President signs and approves the bill. The bill is law.

THE BILL IS LAW

The President can also:

Veto
The President rejects the bill and returns it to Congress with the reasons for the veto. Congress can override the veto with 2/3 vote of those present in both the House and the Senate and the bill will become law.

Choose no action
The President can decide to do nothing. If Congress is in session, after 10 days of no answer from the President, the bill then automatically becomes law.

Pocket veto
If Congress adjourns (goes out of session) within the 10 day period after giving the President the bill, the President can choose not to sign it and the bill will not become law.

Brought to you by usa.gov

Lesson 9

U.S. Constitution, Article II. Executive Branch

A feeble [weak] executive implies a feeble execution of the government. A feeble execution is but another phrase for a bad execution: and a government ill executed, whatever it may be in theory, must be, in practice, a bad government. Those politicians and statesmen who have been the most celebrated for the soundness of their principles, and for the justice of their views, have declared in favour of a single executive and a numerous legislature. They have, with great propriety, considered energy as the most necessary qualification of the former, and have regarded this as most applicable to power in a single hand; while they have, with equal propriety, considered the latter as best adapted to deliberation and wisdom, and best calculated to conciliate the confidence of the people, and to secure their privileges and interests.

Alexander Hamilton, The Federalist No. 70

Compelling Question: The Articles of Confederation had a weak president who presided over the Confederation Congress. How did the increased power of the president under the Constitution improve the functioning of the federal government?

Key Concept

The executive branch of the United States government was created to counterbalance the powers of the legislature. The presidency is structured to

- provide for decisive and unified action in foreign relations and national defense; and
- execute (carry out) domestic laws as passed by Congress.

The President—One Strong Executive

The colonies had been well acquainted with the dangers of monarchy under the English kings Charles I, Charles II, and George III. To avoid tyranny, the delegates to the Second Continental Congress adopted the Articles of Confederation with safeguards against a monarchy by making a weak and plural (divided) executive office. Executive power was spread among representatives of the Confederation Congress. This meant that no one person could effectively enforce the laws passed by the legislature.

In The Federalist No. 70, Alexander Hamilton argues for a strong executive in the Constitution. He writes, "The ingredients which constitute energy in the Executive are, first, unity [one person]; secondly, duration; thirdly, an adequate provision for its support; fourthly, competent powers."

The delegates to the Constitutional Convention agreed on a middle ground between a weak executive and a tyrannical one. The Constitution gives the president the powers necessary to enforce the law but balances this power by providing for his or her impeachment and conviction to prevent the president from becoming a tyrant. The legislative and judicial branches check the president's powers. But the president is to be a strong leader, able to act responsibly as needed. Hamilton writes, "Decision, activity, secrecy, and dispatch will generally characterize the proceedings of one man in a much more eminent degree than the proceedings of any greater number." In other words, he or she must be able to lead the country and make quick decisions when necessary.

George Washington was unanimously selected by the electors to be the first president of the United States. They believed that he would set a precedent for future presidents by his virtuous leadership. They were confident that future presidents would be kept in check by the legislative and judicial branches.

Originally, there were no constitutional limits on how many terms a president could serve. Washington set a precedent for presidents not running for reelection after they had served two terms. The 22nd Amendment, ratified in 1951, established that presidents could be elected for no more than two terms.

Presidential Powers

The president is empowered to operate as the nation's chief executive and takes an oath to preserve, protect, and defend the Constitution. In emergencies, the president can act outside of his or her power to preserve the Constitution. The Constitution provides checks on the president, but debates arise as to what actually constitutes a constitutional crisis, and the limits on presidential power are subject to debate.

Unlike the legislative branch (Congress), which is given only those powers enumerated in the Constitution, the president is given a broader scope of power under the Vesting Clause of Article II. Regarding legislating new laws, the president's power extends only to signing or vetoing bills and enforcing them after they are passed. The Founders established the legislative branch so that the process would be deliberate and careful, requiring time. But they wanted the president to be able to act with speed and decisiveness in making decisions for the country.

While the president does not make law, he or she has the power to sign bills into law or to **veto** (reject) bills he or she finds unconstitutional or unwise. The president sends a vetoed bill back to the house of origin with his or her written objections. Congress can amend the bill and send it back to the president or override the president's veto by a vote of two-thirds of both houses. Laws are not enacted (do not become valid) until they go through the constitutional process. (See "How Does a Bill Become a Law?" in Session 8.)

The president is responsible for implementing and enforcing the laws passed by the legislative branch. So that the president can fulfill this duty, the Constitution in Article II, Section 2, establishes executive departments. The president appoints the department secretaries whose role is to advise the president. President Washington established the precedent of organizing his advisors as the Cabinet, a term not mentioned in the Constitution. Originally, the three members of the president's Cabinet were the secretaries of State, War, and the Treasury.

Over the years, the Cabinet has grown. In the twentieth century, the office of the vice president became more important. Originally, the vice president had few responsibilities. Because the vice president serves as president of the Senate, the office was considered part of the legislative branch. In 1921, President Warren Harding invited Vice President Calvin Coolidge to attend Cabinet meetings and preside in his absence. President Dwight Eisenhower made this practice permanent. Since then, vice presidents have been Cabinet members and are now considered part of the executive branch as well as the legislative branch. He or she must be informed on issues and ready to assume the presidency should the need arise.

Today the Cabinet includes the fifteen secretaries of the following departments: State, Treasury, Defense, Justice, Interior, Agriculture, Commerce, Labor, Health and Human Services, Housing and Urban Development, Transportation, Energy, Education, Veterans Affairs, and Homeland Security. Other members are the White House chief of staff, the U.S. ambassador to the United Nations, and the directors of the Environmental Protection Agency, Office of Management and Budget, U.S. Trade Representative, Small Business Administration, Central Intelligence Agency, Office of the Director of National Intelligence, Office of Science and Technology Policy, and Council of Economic Advisers. The departments and independent federal agencies in the executive branch are responsible for the day-to-day enforcement and administration of federal laws. These departments and agencies have missions and responsibilities as divergent as those of the Department of Defense and the Environmental Protection Agency and the Social Security Administration and the Securities and Exchange Commission. Including members of the armed forces, the executive branch employs more than 4 million people.

One of the president's main roles is **commander in chief** of the nation's military. While the president has the power to command the military and lead the country in times of war, the Constitution prevents the president from abusing these war powers by giving Congress the exclusive power to declare war and fund the military.

Unlike the Articles of Confederation, the Constitution gives the president a general grant of power. He or she has the authority and energy to execute these duties in a decisive way.

Further, the president has the "Power to Grant **Reprieves** and **Pardons** for Offenses against the United States, except in Cases of Impeachment."

As the head of state, the president is primarily responsible for negotiating treaties and alliances. But the president's power to make treaties is checked by the power of the Senate to give advice and consent. Before a treaty becomes law, the senators present must concur by a two-thirds vote. This allows foreign policy and diplomacy to be conducted in a such a way that the United States speaks with one voice in the international community.

Policymaking by the President

The president may advise Congress regarding legislation and has the power to sign bills into law and to veto bills. Over time, however, Congress at times has delegated more and more of its powers to the president. This has resulted in the president taking on powers beyond those that the

Constitution grants the executive branch. In fact, the Constitution specifically grants these powers to the legislative branch.

For example, the House of Representatives is charged with the duty of passing budget bills to fund the government and pay for government programs. Yet the executive branch has taken more and more control of the budget. Another example is the expanding role of the president as commander in chief of the U.S. military, especially in times of war. Although serving as commander in chief is the president's constitutional duty, the Constitution checks the president's power by vesting in Congress the power to declare war and to fund it. Since 1942, however, Congress has not formally declared war. Presidents have led the nation into wars in Korea, Vietnam, Afghanistan, and Iraq, authorized only by congressional resolutions—not declarations of war. Recent debate has raised the question whether Congress has unconstitutionally given up some of its power and deferred to the president.

Executive Orders, Executive Actions, and Executive Memoranda

Executive orders are issued by the president in the *Federal Register* and are used to direct the executive branch of the U.S. government. Executive orders state mandatory requirements and have the effect of law. The Founders did not intend them to be a way to bypass the legislative process, by which Congress adopts major policies. However, presidents have used executive orders increasingly to quickly overturn the policies of previous presidents and bypass Congress. They can be overturned by the Supreme Court.

Executive actions carry none of the weight carried by executive orders. They are informal proposals and directives that are often controversial and sensitive. Executive memoranda are similar to executive orders, having the effect of law yet not published in the *Federal Register*.

Electoral College

The Founders believed that the method of electing the president was critical to maintaining a federal system in which the states have a role and also to maintain a constitutional republic in which citizens have the right to vote. They opposed direct election of the president by **popular vote** because they believed that it would lead to presidential candidates focusing on the issues and interests of a few states with large populations. In a direct popular election, they feared that the small and rural states would be ignored both in the campaign and during the president's term in office. Instead, they favored a system that would discourage the passions of popular mobs and encourage candidates who enjoyed broad support across many states and regions throughout the country.

The Founders thus created the **Electoral College** system, which combines principles of federalism and democracy. Citizens vote for electors who form an Electoral College each presidential election. The candidate who wins a **constitutional majority** is elected. A constitutional majority occurs when one candidate wins a simple majority of 50 percent plus one in a deliberative body such as the Electoral College.

Originally, Article II, Section 1, of the Constitution provided a different method for electing the president and vice president than we use today. Colleges of electors in each state would vote for a candidate. The one who received the most electoral votes would be elected president, and the candidate with the second highest number would be elected vice president. The Founders believed that this process would result in the election of virtuous and well-respected leaders.

The 12th Amendment changed the way the Electoral College functions. Today, citizens vote for a slate of electors in their state who pledge to vote for a particular political party's candidates for president and vice president. Each state has the authority to determine how its electors are apportioned based on how its respective citizens vote. In most states, the candidate who wins the popular vote receives all the state's electoral votes. (Only Maine and Nebraska allocate their electors to reflect the proportion of the popular vote that each candidate receives.) The number of electors is equal to the number of representatives and senators representing the particular state in Congress.

■ Key Terms

Cabinet. A body made up of the heads of the executive departments and others who serve as advisors to the president.

commander in chief. The office the president holds giving him or her supreme command over the country's armed forces.

constitutional majority. One more than half of the members or votes of a deliberative body, such as the Electoral College.

Electoral College. A body of people, called "electors," who represent the states of the United States, and who formally cast votes for the election of the president and vice president.

executive. The leader (president) or branch of government that puts laws into effect and enforces them. In the United States, the executive commands the military, conducts diplomacy, and appoints officials, including federal judges, department heads, and ambassadors.

executive order. A directive issued by the president to manage the operations of the executive branch. It is published in the Federal Register and has the force of law.

impeachment. The constitutional process by which the House of Representatives charges the president or vice president with treason, bribery, or other high crimes or misdemeanors. (The next step is a trial in the Senate, which may vote to convict or not convict. It is only through conviction that the president or vice president [or other civil officer] is removed from office.)

pardon. The official act of a state governor or the U.S. president to forgive a person for a crime with restoration of the full rights of citizenship.

popular vote. The total number of legal votes for a candidate or a ballot issue in an election. The candidate running for U.S. president may not win the election—even after winning the popular vote—if his or her opponent wins the electoral vote.

reprieve. The act of postponing, or giving temporary relief from, the execution of a punishment.

veto. The power of the president to reject bills passed by the legislative branch.

Discussion Questions

1. What are the powers of the executive branch under the U.S. Constitution?

   Executive power is the power of the president to act decisively "to preserve, protect, and defend the Constitution of the United States." The president is to lead the country well, making major decisions in foreign policy and implementing the laws passed by the legislative branch.

2. Why is it important that the executive powers be held by one strong president?

   The executive branch must be effective enough to enforce and execute the laws. The president is able to decisively lead the federal law enforcement agencies and to react appropriately to what is going on in the country. Because the president is one person, he or she is solely responsible for fulfilling the duties of the office. In a body made up of multiple people, such as the legislative branch, it is hard to hold any one person accountable or fix responsibility for poor decisions. It is also hard for a large body to make decisions that need to be quick and decisive. The president can do all these things well and is held accountable because of being entrusted with these duties. He or she is held accountable to the people every four years at election time.

3. What is the extent of the president's war powers?

   The president is the commander in chief of the American military. He or she has the power to command the military at any time. The Constitution specifies that the president's military authority is checked by the legislative branch's power to declare war and its control of the funding for war. In this way, the president ultimately must come to Congress for permission to go to war, even though he or she is the commander in chief of all armed services going into war.

4. Why did the Founders establish the Electoral College to elect the president and vice president?

   The Electoral College (Article II, Section 1, of the Constitution) was intended as a protection of the rights of citizens located in relatively sparsely populated areas of the country. The Electoral College prevents the most populated states from totally dominating the election of the president and vice president. The actual election of the president is based on the established representation of each state in Congress, and this causes candidates to campaign in both urban and rural communities in multiple states—instead of concentrating only on the most densely populated states. In other words, all the country is important—not just the most populous areas. This can be seen as a protection of the rights of a minority in the face of the might of a majority.

Lesson 10

U.S. Constitution, Articles III–VII. Judicial Branch and Implementation of the Constitution

The Constitution ought to be the standard of construction for the laws, and that wherever there is an evident opposition, the laws ought to give place to the Constitution.
Alexander Hamilton, The Federalist No. 81

Compelling Question: How did the Constitution establish a national government that would protect the rights of all citizens while honoring differences between the states?

Key Concepts

1. The Supreme Court is the highest federal court in the United States and takes precedence over all other courts in the nation.

2. The lifetime appointment of judges was intended to ensure the independence of the court, expertise in the law, and the impartial application of the **law** to the facts of specific cases. Under the Constitution, federal judges are to "hold their offices during good behaviour;" their terms do not expire. Their lifetime appointment is to ensure that they are independent in their judgments and apply the law impartially.

3. The U.S. Constitution is the supreme law of the land. It takes precedence over federal, state, and local laws that conflict with it.

4. The Supreme Court decides the constitutionality of the specific cases before it.

5. The goal of the Framers of the Constitution in the Full Faith and Credit Clause was to unite the newborn country while allowing the states to retain some autonomy. To do that, it was necessary to guarantee that judicial decisions and judgments issued by a court in one state would be honored by the courts in any other state.

6. The Constitution provides a formal process to amend the Constitution.

Article III — Judicial Branch

The Constitution (Article III, Section 1) gives **judicial power** to the Supreme Court and any lower courts Congress creates. Currently, there are 94 district (trial) courts and 13 circuit courts (courts of appeal).

Congress sets the number of justices on the Supreme Court. There are now nine justices, including a chief justice. They are nominated by the president "with the advice and consent of the Senate." The president chooses qualified nominees, who must be confirmed by the Senate.

Supreme Court justices are appointed for life with good behavior. This means that justices serve until they retire or upon death. They cannot be removed from office except when impeached and convicted. The lifelong **tenure** of federal district, circuit, and Supreme Court justices promotes the independence of the judiciary from the legislative and executive branches. It also helps ensure that the justices are experts in the law.

The courts interpret questions of law resulting from cases brought to them. The judges and justices decide the merits of a case by interpreting the law and applying it to the particular facts. Judicial review allows justices to ensure that the laws are constitutional.

The Founders anticipated that, even though the Constitution included a Bill of Rights, there would still be assaults on our rights. They gave us a judicial system where citizens could seek justice by filing lawsuits (and provide evidence) in local courts. If a citizen lost the case at this level, he or she could take the case to a higher-level circuit court (court of appeals) in hope of getting justice. If that failed, he or she could file a case with the Supreme Court. In such cases, the Supreme Court can decide to let the decision of the appeals court stand and not consider the case. If it does take the case (it takes fewer than 1 percent of cases submitted), it hears the testimony and considers all evidence and previous court decisions, and then makes a final decision. Decisions by the Supreme Court are of national importance.

Article IV — State Relationships and Powers

Article IV reflects the importance of states in the federal system and helps ensure the rule of law. It defines the relationship between the states and the relationship between the states and the federal government as follows:

1. Judicial decisions and judgments issued by a court in one state are honored by the courts in other states.
2. The privileges and immunities of citizenship must be respected in every state.
3. Congress may admit new states to the union on equal terms.
4. The governments of all states must be republican in form. Each state must be governed by elected officials, have no monarch, and ensure the rule of law.

Article V — Amendment Process

The Founders knew that the country would change over time and that future generations would want to amend parts of the Constitution to reflect the will of the people, correct injustice, and increase freedom. The Founders wanted to ensure that changes were made only after careful deliberation by Congress and state legislatures. They planned a difficult but attainable amendment process. (More than 11,000 amendments have been proposed; only 27 have been ratified by the states.)

Amending the Constitution is a two-step process:

1. Congress proposes and passes an amendment with a two-thirds majority, or two-thirds of the state legislatures vote to have a national constitutional **convention** for proposing amendments.

2. The amendment is ratified by three-fourths of the state legislatures or by conventions in three-fourths of the states. In either process, a **supermajority** (two-thirds) must propose the amendment, and a supermajority of states (three-fourths) must ratify the amendment before it becomes part of the Constitution.

Article VI — Supremacy of the Constitution

Article VI, paragraph 2, of the U.S. Constitution is known as the "Supremacy Clause." It establishes that our Constitution, and federal law generally, take precedence over state laws, and even state constitutions. The Supremacy Clause establishes that the Constitution is the "supreme Law of the Land." The clause requires justices to respect the Constitution and set aside any conflicting laws, declaring them **unconstitutional**. All federal and state public officials must swear an oath to support the Constitution.

Federal laws take precedence over state laws. Federal laws and treaties with other countries signed by the U.S. president are also considered the supreme law of the land. Therefore, they have effect in all the states.

Additionally, Article VI reflects the principle of freedom of religion by forbidding any kind of religious test to "ever be required as a qualification to any office or public trust."

Article VII — Ratification and Signers of the Constitution

Thirty-nine delegates to the Constitutional Convention signed the Constitution on September 17, 1787, before it was sent to the thirteen states for ratification.

The Founders established the process for ratifying the Constitution in Article VII. The U.S. government is based on the consent of the governed. Therefore, they required a higher standard for adopting the Constitution than they had for the Articles of Confederation. The states were required to call state conventions to approve the new form of government. The citizens of each state elected representatives to their state convention for the purpose of debating and voting on the Constitution. Nine states had to ratify the Constitution for it to go into effect. All thirteen original states eventually ratified it. (See Session 12, "Ratification Debates.")

■ Key Terms

convention. A large meeting, or conference, often with delegates who vote on political matters.

judicial power. The power to consider and decide cases and settle disputes of law.

law. A bill passed by the legislative branch, enacted and enforced by the executive branch, open to interpretation by the judicial branch, and adhered to by the citizens.

ratification. The action of signing or giving formal approval to a constitution, amendment, treaty, contract, or agreement, making it officially valid.

supermajority. A number that is much more than half of a total (such as two-thirds or three-fourths), especially in a vote.

tenure. The term during which an office is held.

unconstitutional. In conflict with a constitution.

 Discussion Questions

1. What is judicial power?

   The power to decide cases and settle disputes of law, providing necessary checks and balances to the other branches of government.

2. Define what a law is?

   The rule or order that results from a bill being passed by the legislative branch, then enacted and enforced by the executive branch, open to interpretation by the judicial branch, and adhered to by the citizens.

3. Lifetime appointments for good behavior promote which of the three below?

   a. Entrenched power of the judiciary
   b. The independence of judges and knowledge of the law
   c. An aristocracy of judges

4. The Supreme Court has how many justices?

   a. Three
   b. Nine
   c. Twenty-five

5. What in the Constitution establishes it as the supreme law of the land?

   The Supremacy Clause in Article VI.

6. Supreme Court justices serve for how long?

   a. Five years
   b. Lifetime appointment, assuming good behavior
   c. Twenty years

7. New states will be admitted to the Union on an equal footing.

8. Can the Constitution be legally changed?

   a. No, the Constitution cannot be changed.
   b. Yes, the Constitution can be changed through the amendment process.
   c. Yes, the Constitution can be changed with the unanimous vote of all the states.

9. What is the amendment process?

   a. A simple majority of both houses of Congress can pass amendments and then send them to the president for approval (or veto).
   b. A three-fourths majority of state governors can recommend an amendment and then send it to Congress for ratification.
   c. A two-thirds majority of both houses of Congress may propose an amendment, or two-thirds of the state legislatures may call a convention to propose an amendment. Then three-fourths of the state legislatures or conventions in three-fourths of the states, respectively, must ratify the amendment for it to take effect.

10. Case study: A state has passed a law encroaching on freedom of speech. Obviously, their law conflicts with the First Amendment to the U.S. Constitution. (See Session 13.) The law eventually comes before the U.S. Supreme Court to decide whether or not it is constitutional. How should the Court rule in this case?

    The Constitution is the supreme law of the land. When a state law conflicts with the Constitution, the Constitution prevails. The Supreme Court must declare this new state law unconstitutional.

Lesson 11

Review of the U.S. Constitution

The accumulation of all powers, legislative, executive, and judiciary, in the same hands, whether of one, a few, or many, and whether hereditary, self-appointed, or elective, may justly be pronounced the very definition of tyranny.

James Madison, The Federalist No. 47

Compelling Question: How do the principles of separation of powers, rule of law, and checks and balances work together to prevent any one branch of the government from becoming a tyranny?

Key Concepts

1. The Founders designed the Constitution based on the essential principle of separation of powers. Each of the three branches of government has its own specific purpose. Each branch is restricted from encroaching on the responsibilities of the other branches.

2. Rule of law is the doctrine that all people and institutions are subject to the same laws and regulations without regard to their access to the power of government.

3. Checks and balances describes the means by which each of the three branches of government protects its own roles and responsibilities while also preventing the expansion of powers in the other two branches.

The Importance of Separation of Powers

The colonists rebelled against Great Britain because the British ruled them without their consent and violated their natural rights. The colonists expected to be treated as fairly as Englishmen would be in London. When it was clear that King George III and Parliament would not do so, they established a new nation that would defend the rights of the American people. But the revolution would not serve freedom and liberty if the new American government would be just another monarchy. The Founders chose to craft a new Constitution that would ensure that the government was accountable to the people.

The well-read Founders had learned from history that a characteristic of tyrannical governments was that they never separated the powers of government. The Founders created three branches of government so that they would have to answer to one another for their actions. The legislative branch is to make laws, the executive branch is to enforce laws, and the judicial branch is to interpret laws and make sure the Constitution is upheld. They knew that humans are naturally self-interested. People are prone to pass laws that benefit themselves and not for the common good. Most people cannot be trusted to fairly judge their own actions. The **separation of powers** ensures that our government is accountable to the people and that different people are responsible for making, enforcing, and judging laws.

The Rule of Law and Why It Is Important

The **rule of law** is the principle that both government and all the governed are subject to the law. And that all are to be treated the same way by the law. It means that the rules apply to everyone in the same manner, regardless of his or her status, power, race, or age. This cornerstone of our republic seeks to stop the arbitrary judgment of government officials. John Adams famously described the purpose of the Constitution as ensuring that the government will be "a government of laws, and not of men."

Adams and the other Founders knew well what happened when there was no rule of law, such as in the last years of the Roman Empire. The emperor enacted laws that he wanted—even when they violated the rights of the people. He created different rules for different groups without prior notice. The people had no court they could bring their case to. Their only recourse was to appeal to the emperor. But as an all-powerful tyrant, he killed citizens and took their property. He was above any law. He was the law unto himself. They could not stop him by bringing their case before a court.

In contrast, the U.S. Constitution guarantees that the abuses such as those of the Roman emperor—or of King George III—cannot happen in the United States, where the laws are to apply equally to all citizens. In the United States, all laws must be passed by a legislature accountable to the people. If Congress passes an unconstitutional law, the people can elect new senators and representatives. Or they can appeal to the courts to strike down laws. If the president enforces a law unfairly, the people can elect a new president. Or they can (1) appeal to a court to have the law enforced fairly, (2) appeal to Congress to clarify the meaning of the law, or (3) in extreme cases, impeach and convict the president by actions of the House and Senate.

How Separation of Powers and the Rule of Law Are Related

If there were no separation of powers, there would be little respect for the law since the enforcement of the law would not be checked by anyone other than the ruler or president. He or she could violate the rights of citizens and not have to answer for it. But the Constitution ensures that there is no concentration of power in one branch or individual. The branches each have separate functions: Congress passes legislation, the president enacts and enforces laws, and the federal courts judge the laws.

The Constitution ensures that the laws are supreme. Each branch of government can protect against another branch violating the law. Each branch of government is accountable to the Constitution—the supreme law of the land.

The Difference between Separation of Powers and Checks and Balances

Separation of Powers refers to the powers of government—passing legislation, enforcing laws, and judging laws—being distributed between the three branches. Congress is the only branch that can pass laws, the executive is the only branch that can enforce laws, and the judiciary is the only branch that can judge disputes arising under the law.

Checks and balances refers to how the branches of government are accountable to one another. Specific powers are granted to each branch to prevent and challenge abuses of power by other branches. The president, for example, has the power to veto laws passed by Congress. The veto allows the president to protect his or her own powers. Or the president could veto a bill passed by Congress that would deny the president the money to pay for the armed forces. The veto also provides the president with a means to reject bills believed to be unconstitutional prior to Supreme Court review. The House of Representatives can impeach a president who violates his or her constitutional duties, and the Senate can convict him or her. The courts can strike down unconstitutional laws.

Defending the Constitution

Every member of the federal government—senators and representatives, the president, judges, and federal employees alike—swear an oath to defend the Constitution. They are all responsible for defending the meaning of the Constitution but do so in different ways. When proposing legislation, our elected officials should debate whether it is constitutional. Congress should repeal laws that are unconstitutional. The president should veto bills passed by Congress that he or she believes are unconstitutional.

The courts' power is key to resolving disputes about the law. Because the Constitution is the supreme law of the land, the district courts, circuit (appeals) courts, and the Supreme Court must strike down any law that conflicts with the Constitution. If a case is not settled in the lower courts and it ends up in the Supreme Court, the nine justices make the final determination. The Supreme Court justices often disagree about the original intent of the legislation or whether it is constitutional. For example, in many cases, five justices agree with the **plaintiff**, and four vote for the **defendant**—and vice versa.

Ultimately, the people must take an interest in their government, be aware of efforts to violate the Constitution, and work to elect senators, representatives, and a president who uphold it. For example, many Americans believed that the Alien and Sedition Acts passed in the 1790s were unconstitutional. But they did not rely on the court to strike them down. Rather, in the election of 1800, the American people overwhelmingly voted for Thomas Jefferson's Democratic Republicans, who promised to undo the Alien and Sedition Acts. Today, voters can elect presidents who will nominate Supreme Court justices who have a record of either interpreting the Constitution by what the Founders intended or who believe that the Constitution is a "living document" to be interpreted according to current public opinion.

Understanding the Intent of the Founders

Alexander Hamilton, James Madison, and John Jay, three prominent Federalists, wrote a series of articles published in New York City newspapers. These articles explained to citizens what the various provisions of the proposed Constitution meant. The authors' purpose was to encourage adoption of the Constitution by the convention formed in New York State. The individual articles were later collected into what is now called *The Federalist Papers*, commonly known as *The Federalist*. This collection of articles is considered the best explanation of why and how the Constitution should work. While not considered an organic law of the American Government, *The Federalist* is widely held as a foundational document.

■ Key Terms

checks and balances. The principle, or system, in the U.S. Constitution in which each separate branch of the government has some power to check (change or overturn) some actions by the other two branches. The purpose is to provide balance among the branches and to ensure that political power is not concentrated in the hands of any individual or group so that no branch of government becomes too powerful.

defendant. The person or entity being sued in a court of law.

plaintiff. The person or entity filing a lawsuit against the defendant in a court of law.

rule of law. The principle that all people and institutions are subject to and accountable to law that is fairly applied and enforced; the principle of government by law.

separation of powers. The principle that each of the three branches of government— legislative, executive, and judicial—has well-defined roles, responsibilities, and authority to act, which are prescribed by the Constitution so that no branch may assume the powers of the other branches.

Discussion Questions

1. What are the purposes of the Constitution?

    a. To form a more perfect union
    b. To establish justice
    c. To ensure domestic tranquility
    d. To provide for the Common Defense
    e. To promote the General Welfare
    f. To secure the blessings of liberty to ourselves and our posterity

2. What are some of the legislative powers granted to Congress by the Constitution? How does each legislative power promote one or more of the Constitution's purposes?

    1. To lay (impose) and collect taxes
    2. To regulate international commerce
    3. To establish a uniform rule of naturalization
    4. To coin money and regulate its value
    5. To provide for the punishment of counterfeiting
    6. To establish post offices and roads

7. To establish federal courts lower than the Supreme Court
8. To declare war
9. To raise and support armies and provide and maintain a navy
10. To provide for the calling out of the militia to execute laws of the union, suppress insurrections, and repel invasion

3. Suppose that Congress decided to grant its power to make laws and the court's power to judge the constitutionality of laws wholly to the president. Why would this be a problem?

   There would be no checks and balances or separation of power to stop the president from being tyrannical.

4. What does it mean for the Constitution to be the Supreme Law of the Land?

   The Constitution takes precedence over the laws in all cities, counties, states, and territories. Every law must be in accord with the Constitution. If a law conflicts with the Constitution, it must be repealed by Congress or struck down by the Supreme Court.

5. How can you defend the Constitution?

   Our Founders expected citizens to be informed about our constitutional republic and the Constitution so that they would have sufficient knowledge to notice threats to the United States and protect it against "all enemies, foreign and domestic." Key to this is electing virtuous men and women to positions of power, at all levels but especially to the Congress, state and local courts, and office of president. We must support good government and defend the Constitution by working for justice consistent with the principles of the American government as adopted by the Founders. And we must do our duty to vote in elections based on knowledge of the issues.

6. What can the American people do if the government is not upholding the Constitution?

   They can elect a new president, new senators, new representatives, and other government officials who promise to either repeal or change the unconstitutional law. They can replace the elected officials who do not uphold the Constitution, sometimes getting candidates to promise how they would vote before the election.

Lesson 12

Ratification Debates

A dependence on the people is, no doubt, the primary control on the government, but experience has taught mankind the necessity of auxiliary precautions.

James Madison, The Federalist No. 51

Compelling Question: The debate over whether to ratify the new Constitution happened between those who argued in its favor (the Federalists) and those who argued against it (the Anti-Federalists). How well did the Federalists address the concerns of the Anti-Federalists?

Key Concepts

The Articles of Confederation, our first constitution, was weak, so the Founders replaced it with the U.S. Constitution eight years later. The weaknesses of the Articles of Confederation government led to the Constitutional Convention in Philadelphia in 1787.

1. The modern concept of a valid **republican** form of government includes separation of powers, checks and balances, elected representatives, and an independent judiciary.

2. The principle of separation of powers was established by the Founders to divide the three main functions of government into individual branches.

3. *The Federalist* advocated for ratification of the new Constitution by publicly addressing the concerns of leaders opposed to it: the Anti-Federalists.

Ratification Debates

When the four-month-long Constitutional Convention ended, some doubted whether the Constitution would be accepted by all the states. The ratification plan required that representatives be elected to state conventions to debate and vote on the document. Nine states had to ratify the Constitution before it could form the basis for a new federal government.

At the ratification conventions, particularly in Virginia and New York, the delegates hotly debated issues in the Constitution. The Federalists advocated for the Constitution, and the Anti-Federalists opposed it in spirited debates in newspapers, meetings, and homes throughout the states.

Three prominent Federalists Alexander Hamilton, James Madison, and John Jay wrote essays known as "*The Federalist Papers*," or *"The Federalist."* They argued in favor of the improvements the new Constitution would provide. These essays, published in a series of New York newspapers in 1787–1788, are considered the best explanation of the principles and government structure defined in the Constitution and how it was intended to operate.

We focus on two of the most important of them: Federalist 10 and 51. In Federalist 10, Madison contends that a large republic with a system of representation will prevent the tyranny of factions, which are groups of citizens with similar interests that may oppress the rights of minorities or the public good. He claims that a federal system, which divides power between a central government and constituent states, is the best solution to the problem of factions.

Federalist No. 51 is an essay by Madison that advocates a separation of powers within the national government1. The essay explains how the new constitution will prevent departments of the government from intruding into each others' domains, besides giving citizens the power to prevent their elected representatives from abusing their powers. Madison emphasizes the need for checks and balances through the separation of powers into three branches of the federal government and the division of powers between the federal government and the states.

(The complete texts of "The Federalist 10" and "The Federalist 51" are included at the end of this lesson.)

Disadvantages of the Articles of Confederation

The Constitution corrected the main weaknesses of the Articles of Confederation, including:
- An executive too weak to enforce laws
- Congress's inability to directly raise taxes to meet expenses
- No independent judiciary
- Difficulty passing legislation (requiring nine states to agree)

During the Revolutionary War, the ineffectiveness of the Articles of Confederation had reached a crisis. The Articles provided no way to supply the Continental Army serving under General George Washington. The troops suffered from a lack of food, shelter, clothing, and other supplies. And they were compensated little or not at all.

The failure of the Confederation Congress to pay ex-soldiers what they were owed for their wartime service had widespread consequences. It made it impossible for veterans (now farmers) to make good on their own private debts, including taxes! Following the war, New England had not yet recovered from the loss of business and trade with Great Britain. Merchants and local governments were hurting financially and needed to be paid, so they sued the veterans and deprived them of their property or liberty by putting them in prison. In response, Daniel Shays and other veterans attacked courthouses and government property. Shays' Rebellion (1786–1787) and other smaller movements led Federalists to charge that the United States had become vulnerable to rule by the mob, so they lobbied for a stronger federal government.

Delegates from five states assembled in Annapolis, Maryland, to discuss promoting interstate commerce, but they instead called for a general convention to propose amendments to the Articles of Confederation. But the need for a new government became abundantly clear. Eight years under the Articles of Confederation proved that the Founders needed to devise a stronger government consistent with the republican form of government. So, in 1787, delegates from all the states assembled in Philadelphia to write the Constitution.

Advantages of the Constitution

The Federalists drew on their deep knowledge of ancient and medieval history and their understanding of Enlightenment thought to design a unique system of government, a constitutional republic grounded on the natural rights of man and the consent of the governed.

They knew that **direct democracies** historically did not endure long because of two main flaws. The first was tyranny of the majority, which trampled on the rights of the minority. The second was the common tendency of direct democracies to divide into fierce factions and to descend into mob rule. Ultimately, they failed because of civil war or conquest by another nation.

Because of these flaws, the Founders established a republican form of government in the Constitution that would respect the rule of law and protect the rights of all citizens, including those in the minority. The concept of the constitutional republic developed by the Founders includes these key elements:

- Separation of powers, which guards against one man or group dominating all others
- Representatives, including the president, senators, and members of the House of Representatives, selected by the people to reflect the consent of the governed
- An **independent judiciary** with judges serving lifetime appointments so that they are not subject to political pressure and are better able to provide an impartial application of the law
- A system of checks and balances that allows each branch to protect its own powers and prevent the other branches from overstepping their powers
- Any defects of a republican form of government could be overcome because of our system of checks and balances, separation of powers, and the amendment process.

Federalism, dividing the power between the federal government and the states, is an especially important way to protect liberty. By reserving all powers not specifically delegated to the federal government to the individual states, the federal government is restricted from exceeding its vested powers. The federal system empowers states to solve their own issues.

By providing a means for the citizens to select their own representatives, both by popular election and, originally, through the states' selection of senators, the Constitution promotes public debate and deliberation. By dispersing the authority and power to pass and then enact legislation, such an arrangement encourages factions to achieve a broad consensus on issues.

America's Founders were in favor of a society that practiced democratic ideals but were opposed to government by direct democracy. Alexander Hamilton was the main author of *The Federalist*, the first Secretary of the U.S. Treasury, and a student of ancient history. In his speech to the U.S. Constitution Ratifying Convention in New York on June 21, 1788, he warned lawmakers:

> It has been observed that a pure democracy if it were practicable would be the most perfect government. Experience has proved that no position is more false than this. The ancient democracies in which the people themselves deliberated never possessed one good feature of government. Their very character was tyranny.

James Madison is known as the "Father of the U.S. Constitution." He served as the fourth U.S. president. His essays in *The Federalist* warned against the lawlessness that proceeds from collective rights (rather than individual rights). In *The Federalist No. 10*, he writes:

> Democracy is the most vile form of government . . . Democracies have ever been spectacles of turbulence and contention: have ever been found incompatible with personal security or the rights of property: and have in general been as short in their lives as they have been violent in their deaths.

And in *The Federalist No. 55*, Madison writes, "Had every Athenian citizen been a Socrates, every Athenian assembly would still have been a mob."

The Anti-Federalists Concerns about the Constitution

The Anti-Federalists originally opposed the Constitution. Their members included prominent revolutionaries, such as Patrick Henry of Virginia and Samuel Adams of Massachusetts. They had several complaints against the new form of government. Anti-Federalists worried that the new Constitution
- Was not responsive enough to the people;
- Established a national judiciary, independent of states' control;
- Made no mention or allowance for term limits on office holders; and
- Did not provide for enough representatives of the people in Congress.

History included examples of republics that had been successful for relatively small populations. The intended union of the United States, however, would be large, and this concerned them. They advocated for more elected representatives, for term limits, and for the frequent rotation of officeholders. Some Anti-Federalists feared that the Constitution gave too much power to the president. Others worried that Article III would result in judicial tyranny because federal judges would have lifetime appointments.

Progress was made in adopting the Constitution with the support of the Anti-Federalists because the Federalists promised to provide a bill of rights after the Constitution was ratified. These safeguards of liberty to all were added as amendments one through ten and sent to the states for ratification by President Washington.

Founders' Biographies—Alexander Hamilton, James Madison, and John Jay

Each of the following men played key roles in our nation's founding, and each contributed essays to *The Federalist*.

Alexander Hamilton (1755–1804), an orphan, immigrated to America from the island of Nevis in the West Indies. He studied at King's College (today's Columbia University). During the American Revolution, he served as George Washington's senior aide, and commanded troops in battle at the American victory at Yorktown. When the war ended, Hamilton became a lawyer, served in the Confederation Congress, and was a member of the Constitutional Convention. He served as the first Secretary of the Treasury under George Washington. He was killed in a duel with Aaron Burr.

James Madison (1751–1836) from Virginia served in the Continental Congress and was influential in the Constitutional Convention. He served in the first Congress under the U.S. Constitution and helped frame the Bill of Rights, working hard to ensure it passed. He and Thomas Jefferson were the founders of the Democratic-Republican Party. Under President Jefferson, he served as secretary of state until the day before being inaugurated as the fourth president in 1809.

John Jay (1745–1829) was a New Yorker with extensive experience in government. He served in the Continental Congress, assisted in drafting the New York constitution, and was secretary of foreign affairs under the Articles of Confederation after the end of the American Revolution. He later served as Chief Justice of the United States Supreme Court and governor of New York.

■ Key Terms

direct democracy. Direct rule by the people, rather than by elected representatives.

independent judiciary. A judiciary system that is separate from and not controlled by either the legislative or executive branch.

republican. Relating to a system of government, such as in the United States and individual states, in which legal voters elect the head of state (president or governor) and legislators. The people and their elected representatives are the source of power in the government.

Discussion Questions

1. Why is it important for the Constitution to require separation of powers between the branches?

   Separation of powers is important because it is intended that no one branch of the government can become too strong and dominate the others. The Founders assumed that each branch of the federal government would vigilantly guard their authorized powers against encroachment by the others.

2. What are the advantages of the Constitution?

   a. Representatives elected by the people
   b. Process to add new states to the union
   c. An independent judiciary
   d. Checks and balances
   e. Separation of powers
   f. No aristocracy
   g. One strong executive

3. Who wrote *The Federalist Papers*?

   Alexander Hamilton, James Madison, and John Jay

4. Why did the Anti-Federalists oppose the Constitution?

   The Anti-Federalists opposed the Constitution because they thought it made the federal government too strong. They argued that the power of the states would be weakened by an unduly strong executive branch; that the lack of term limits would lead to an unresponsive Congress and presidency; and that an independent judiciary with life tenure would lead to tyranny. Some Anti-Federalists, however, were satisfied by promises to add a bill of rights.

5. Why did Hamilton, Madison, and Jay write *The Federalist*?

   They wrote *The Federalist* essays to explain the Constitution, to persuade the New York convention delegates to vote for the Constitution, and to counter the arguments of the Anti-Federalists.

6. What is federalism?

   Federalism is a system of government in which power is divided between the federal government and the states. This division of power is a main organizational method of protecting the liberty of citizens. The Founders knew the dangers of centralized power, so they carefully vested the powers given to the federal branches of government. They further checked the powers of the federal government by stating that the rest of the powers remained with the states and ultimately the people.

7. What does *direct democracy* mean?

   Direct democracy—in contrast to representative democracy—is unqualified majority rule. Often in assemblies, voters elect their leaders and pass all their laws by at least one vote more than half of the votes. The rights of those in the minority are not protected. The Founders were wary of direct democracies because they could end in mob rule.

8. Who holds the powers not given to the federal government in the Constitution?

   The states and ultimately the people hold the powers not given to the federal government in the Constitution. The Constitution creates an effective yet limited federal government based on the powers vested in each branch. The only powers the federal government possesses are those delegated to it in the Constitution. The powers of the states, like those of the federal government, depend on the consent of the governed.

THE FEDERALIST NUMBER 10

[22 November 1787]

The Size and Variety of the Union as A Check on Faction

To the People of the State of New York:

Among the numerous advantages promised by a well-constructed Union, none deserves to be more accurately developed than its tendency to break and control the violence of faction. The friend of popular governments never finds himself so much alarmed for their character and fate, as when he contemplates their propensity to this dangerous vice. He will not fail, therefore, to set a due value on any plan which, without violating the principles to which he is attached, provides a proper cure for it. The instability, injustice, and confusion introduced into the public councils, have, in truth, been the mortal diseases under which popular governments have everywhere perished; as they continue to be the favorite and fruitful topics from which the adversaries to liberty derive their most specious declamations. The valuable improvements made by the American constitutions on the popular models, both ancient and modern, cannot certainly be too much admired; but it would be an unwarrantable partiality, to contend that they have as effectually obviated the danger on this side, as was wished and expected. Complaints are everywhere heard from our most considerate and virtuous citizens, equally the friends of public and private faith, and of public and personal liberty, that our governments are too unstable, that the public good disregarded in the conflicts of rival parties, and that measures are too often decided, not according to the rules of justice and the rights of the minor party, but by the superior force of an interested and overbearing majority. However anxiously we may wish that these complaints had no foundation, the evidence of known facts will not permit us to deny that they are in some degree true. It will be found indeed, on a candid review of our situation, that some of the distresses under which we labour, have been erroneously charged on the operation of our governments; but it will be found at the same time, that other causes will not alone account for many of our heaviest misfortunes; and particularly, for that prevailing and increasing distrust of public engagements, and alarm for private rights, which are echoed from one end of the continent to the other. These must be chiefly, if not wholly, effects of the unsteadiness and injustice, with which a factious spirit has tainted our public administration.

By a faction I understand a number of citizens, whether amounting to a majority or minority of the whole, who are united and actuated by some common impulse of passion, or of interest, adverse to the rights of other citizens, or to the permanent and aggregate interests of the community.

There are two methods of curing the mischiefs of faction: The one, by removing its causes; the other, by controlling its effects.

There are again two methods of removing the causes of faction: The one by destroying the liberty which is essential to its existence; the other, by giving to every citizen the same opinions, the same passions, and the same interests.

It could never be more truly said than of the first remedy, that it is worse than the disease. Liberty is to faction, what air is to fire, an aliment without which it instantly expires. But it could not be a less folly to abolish liberty, which is essential to political life, because it nourishes faction, than it would be to wish the annihilation of air, which is essential to animal life because it imparts to fire its destructive agency.

The second expedient is as impracticable, as the first would be unwise. As long as the reason of man continues fallible, and he is at liberty to exercise it, different opinions will be formed. As long as the connection subsists between his reason and his self-love, his opinions and his passions will have a reciprocal influence on each other; and the former will be objects to which the latter will attach themselves. The diversity in the faculties of men from which the rights of property originate, is not less an insuperable obstacle to an uniformity of interests. The protection of these faculties is the first object of government. From the protection of different and unequal faculties of acquiring property, the possession of different degrees and kinds of property immediately results: And from the influence of these on the sentiments and views of the respective proprietors, ensues a division of the society into different interests and parties.

The latent causes of faction are thus sown in the nature of man; and we see them every where brought into different degrees of activity, according to the different circumstances of civil society. A zeal for different opinions concerning religion, concerning government, and many other points, as well of speculation as of practice; an attachment to different leaders ambitiously contending for pre-eminence and power; or to persons of other descriptions whose fortunes have been interesting to the human passions, have in turn divided mankind into parties, inflamed them with mutual animosity, and rendered them much more disposed to vex and oppress each other, than to co-operate for their common good. So strong is this propensity of mankind to fall into mutual animosities, that where no substantial occasion presents itself, the most frivolous and fanciful distinctions have been sufficient to kindle their unfriendly passions, and excite their most violent conflicts. But the most common and durable source of factions, has been the various and unequal distribution of property. Those who hold, and those who are without property, have ever formed distinct interests in society. Those who are creditors and those who are debtors, fall under a like discrimination. A landed interest, a manufacturing interest, a mercantile interest, a monied interest, with many lesser interests, grow up of necessity in civilized nations, and divide them into different classes, actuated by different sentiments and views. The regulation of these various and interfering interests forms the principal task of modern legislation, and involves the spirit of party and faction in the necessary and ordinary operations of government.

No man is allowed to be a judge in his own cause; because his interest would certainly bias his judgment, and, not improbably, corrupt his integrity. With equal, nay with greater reason, a body of men, are unfit to be both judges and parties, at the same time; yet, what are many of the most important acts of legislation, but so many judicial determinations, not indeed concerning the rights of single persons, but concerning the rights of large bodies of citizens; and what are the different classes of legislators, but advocates and parties to the causes which they determine? Is a law proposed concerning private debts? It is a question to which the creditors are parties on one side, and the debtors on the other. Justice ought to hold the balance between them. Yet the parties are and must be themselves the judges; and the most numerous party, or, in other words, the most powerful faction must be expected to prevail. Shall domestic manufacturers be encouraged, and in what degree, by restrictions on foreign manufactures? Are questions which would be differently decided by the landed and the manufacturing classes; and probably by neither, with a sole regard to justice and the public good. The apportionment of taxes on the various descriptions of property, is an act which seems to require the most exact impartiality, yet there is perhaps no legislative act in which greater opportunity and temptation are given to a predominant party, to trample on the rules of justice. Every shilling with which they over-burden the inferior number, is a shilling saved to their own pockets.

It is vain to say, that enlightened statesmen will be able to adjust these clashing interests, and render them all subservient to the public good. Enlightened statesmen will not always be at the helm: Nor, in many cases, can such an adjustment be made at all, without taking into view indirect and remote considerations, which will rarely prevail over the immediate interest which one party may find in disregarding the rights of another, or the good of the whole.

The inference to which we are brought, is, that the causes of faction cannot be removed; and that relief is only to be sought in the means of controlling its effects.

If a faction consists of less than a majority, relief is supplied by the republican principle, which enables the majority to defeat its sinister views by regular vote: It may clog the administration, it may convulse the society; but it will be unable to execute and mask its violence under the forms of the constitution. When a majority is included in a faction, the form of popular government on the other hand enables it to sacrifice to its ruling passion or interest, both public good and the rights of other citizens. To secure the public good, and private rights against the danger of such a faction, and at the same time to preserve the spirit and the form of popular government, is then the great object to which our enquiries are directed. Let me add that it is the great desideratum, by which alone this form of government can be rescued from the opprobrium, under which it has so long labored, and be recommended to the esteem and adoption of mankind.

By what means is this object attainable? Evidently by one of two only. Either the existence of the same passion or interest in a majority at the same time, must be prevented; or the majority, having such co-existent passion or interest, must be rendered, by their number and local situation, unable to concert and carry into effect schemes of oppression. If the impulse and the opportunity be suffered to coincide, we well know that neither moral nor religious motives can be relied on as an adequate control. They are not found to be such on the injustice and violence of individuals, and lose their efficacy in proportion to the number combined together; that is, in proportion as their efficacy becomes needful.

From this view of the subject, it may be concluded that a pure democracy, by which I mean a society, consisting of a small number of citizens, who assemble and administer the government in person, can admit of no cure for the mischiefs of faction. A common passion or interest will, in almost every case, be felt by a majority of the whole; a communication and concert results from the form of government itself; and there is nothing to check the inducements to sacrifice the weaker party, or an obnoxious individual. Hence it is, that such democracies have ever been spectacles of turbulence and contention; have ever been found incompatible with personal security, or the rights of property; and have in general been as short in their lives, as they have been violent in their deaths. Theoretic politicians, who have patronized this species of government, have erroneously supposed, that by reducing mankind to perfect equality in their political rights, they would, at the same time, be perfectly equalized, and assimilated in their possessions, their opinions, and their passions.

A republic, by which I mean a government in which the scheme of representation takes place, opens a different prospect, and promises the cure for which we are seeking. Let us examine the points in which it varies from pure democracy, and we shall comprehend both the nature of the cure, and the efficacy which it must derive from the union.

The two great points of difference between a democracy and a republic, are first, the delegation of the government, in the latter, to a small number of citizens elected by the rest; secondly, the greater number of citizens, and greater sphere of country, over which the latter may be extended.

The effect of the first difference is, on the one hand, to refine and enlarge the public views, by passing them through the medium of a chosen body of citizens, whose wisdom may best discern the true interest of their country, and whose patriotism and love of justice, will be least likely to sacrifice it to temporary or partial considerations. Under such a regulation, it may well happen that the public voice pronounced by the representatives of the people, will be more consonant to the public good, than if pronounced by the people themselves convened for the purpose. On the other hand, the effect may be inverted. Men of factious tempers, of local prejudices, or of sinister designs, may by intrigue, by corruption, or by other means, first obtain the suffrages, and then betray the interests of the people. The question resulting is, whether small or extensive republics are most favourable to the election of proper guardians of the public weal; and it is clearly decided in favour of the latter by two obvious considerations.

In the first place it is to be remarked, that however small the republic may be, the representatives must be raised to a certain number, in order to guard against the cabals of a few; and that however large it may be, they must be limited to a certain number, in order to guard against the confusion of a multitude. Hence the number of representatives in the two cases note being in proportion to that of the constituents, and being proportionally greatest in the small republic, it follows, that if the proportion of fit characters be not less in the large than in the small republic, the former will present a greater option, and consequently a greater probability of a fit choice.

In the next place, as each representative will be chosen by greater number of citizens in the large than in the small republic, it will be more difficult for unworthy candidates to practise with success the vicious arts, by which elections are too often carried; and the suffrages of the people being more free, will be more likely to centre on men who possess the most attractive merit, and the most diffusive and established characters.

It must be confessed, that in this, as in most other cases, there is a mean, on both sides of which inconveniencies will be found to lie. By enlarging too much the number of electors, you render the representative too little acquainted with all their local circumstances and lesser interests; as by reducing it too much, you render him unduly attached to these, and too little fit to comprehend and pursue great and national objects. The federal constitution forms a happy combination in this respect; the great and aggregate interests being referred to the national, the local and particular to the state legislatures.

The other point of difference is, the greater number of citizens and extent of territory which may be brought within the compass of republican, than of democratic government; and it is this circumstance principally which renders factious combinations less to be dreaded in the former, than in the latter. The smaller the society, the fewer probably will be the distinct parties and interests composing it; the fewer the distinct parties and interests, the more frequently will a majority be found in the same party; and the smaller the number of individuals composing a majority, and the smaller the compass within which they are placed, the more easily will they concert and execute their plans of oppression. Extend the sphere, and you take in a greater variety of parties and interests; you make it less probable that a majority of the whole will have a common motive to invade the rights of other citizens; or if such a common motive exists, it will be more difficult for all who feel it to discover their own strength, and to act in unison with each other. Besides other impediments, it may be remarked, that where there is a consciousness of unjust or dishonourable purposes, communication is always checked by distrust, in proportion to the number whose concurrence is necessary.

Hence it clearly appears, that the same advantage, which a republic has over a democracy, in controlling the effects of faction, is enjoyed by a large over a small republic—is enjoyed by the union over the states composing it. Does this advantage consist in the substitution of representatives, whose enlightened views and virtuous sentiments render them superior to local prejudices, and to schemes of injustice? It will not be denied, that the representation of the union will be most likely to possess these requisite endowments. Does it consist in the greater security afforded by a greater variety of parties, against the event of any one party being able to outnumber and oppress the rest? In an equal degree does the encreased variety of parties, comprised within the union, encrease this security. Does it, in fine, consist in the greater obstacles opposed to the concert and accomplishment of the secret wishes of an unjust and interested majority? Here, again, the extent of the union gives it the most palpable advantage.

The influence of factious leaders may kindle a flame within their particular states, but will be unable to spread a general conflagration through the other states: A religious sect, may degenerate into a political faction in a part of the confederacy; but the variety of sects dispersed over the entire face of it, must secure the national councils against any danger from that source: a rage for paper money, for an abolition of debts, for an equal division of property, or for any other improper or wicked project, will be less apt to pervade the whole body of the union, than a particular member of it; in the same proportion as such a malady is more likely to taint a particular county or district, than an entire state.

In the extent and proper structure of the union, therefore, we behold a republican remedy for the diseases most incident to republican government. And according to the degree of pleasure and pride, we feel in being republicans, ought to be our zeal in cherishing the spirit, and supporting the character of federalists.

Publius [James Madison]

Madison, James. "The Federalist Number 10." [22 November] 1787. *Founders Online*. National Archives. https://founders.archives.gov/documents/Madison/01-10-02-0178.

Madison, James. "10 The Size and Variety of the Union as a Check on Faction." Edited by Benjamin Fletcher Wright. *The Federalist*. New York: Barnes and Noble Books, 1961.

THE FEDERALIST NUMBER 51

[6 February 1788]

Checks and Balances

To the people of the State of New York:

To what expedient then shall we finally resort for maintaining in practice the necessary partition of power among the several departments, as laid down in the constitution? The only answer that can be given is, that as all these exterior provisions are found to be inadequate, the defect must be supplied, by so contriving the interior structure of the government, as that its several constituent parts may, by their mutual relations, be the means of keeping each other in their proper places. Without presuming to undertake a full development of this important idea, I will hazard a few general observations, which may perhaps place it in a clearer light, and enable us to form a more correct judgment of the principles and structure of the government planned by the convention.

In order to lay a due foundation for that separate and distinct exercise of the different powers of government, which to a certain extent, is admitted on all hands to be essential to the preservation of liberty, it is evident that each department should have a will of its own; and consequently should be so constituted, that the members of each should have as little agency as possible in the appointment of the members of the others. Were this principle rigorously adhered to, it would require that all the appointments for the supreme executive, legislative, and judiciary magistracies, should be drawn from the same fountain of authority, the people, through channels, having no communication whatever with one another. Perhaps such a plan of constructing the several departments would be less difficult in practice than it may in contemplation appear. Some difficulties, however, and some additional expence, would attend the execution of it. Some deviations therefore from the principle must be admitted. In the constitution of the judiciary department in particular, it might be inexpedient to insist rigorously on the principle; first, because peculiar qualifications being essential in the members, the primary consideration ought to be to select that mode of choice, which best secures these qualifications; secondly, because the permanent tenure by which the appointments are held in that department, must soon destroy all sense of dependence on the authority conferring them.

It is equally evident that the members of each department should be as little dependent as possible on

those of the others, for the emoluments annexed to their offices. Were the executive magistrate, or the judges, not independent of the legislature in this particular, their independence in every other would be merely nominal.

But the great security against a gradual concentration of the several powers in the same department, consists in giving to those who administer each department, the necessary constitutional means, and personal motives, to resist encroachments of the others. The provision for defence must in this, as in all other cases, be made commensurate to the danger of attack. Ambition must be made to counteract ambition. The interest of the man must be connected with the constitutional rights of the place. It may be a reflection on human nature, that such devices should be necessary to control the abuses of government. But what is government itself but the greatest of all reflections on human nature? If men were angels, no government would be necessary. If angels were to govern men, neither external nor internal controls on government would be necessary. In framing a government which is to be administered by men over men, the great difficulty lies in this: You must first enable the government to controul the governed; and in the next place, oblige it to controul itself. A dependence on the people is no doubt the primary controul on the government; but experience has taught mankind the necessity of auxiliary precautions. This policy of supplying by opposite and rival interests, the defect of better motives, might be traced through the whole system of human affairs, private as well as public. We see it particularly displayed in all the subordinate distributions of power; where the constant aim is to divide and arrange the several offices in such a manner as that each may be a check on the other; that the private interest of every individual, may be a centinel over the public rights. These inventions of prudence cannot be less requisite in the distribution of the supreme powers of the state.

But it is not possible to give to each department an equal power of self defence. In republican government the legislative authority, necessarily, predominates. The remedy for this inconveniency is, to divide the legislature into different branches; and to render them by different modes of election, and different principles of action, as little connected with each other, as the nature of their common functions, and their common dependence on the society, will admit. It may even be necessary to guard against dangerous encroachments by still further precautions. As the weight of the legislative authority requires that it should be thus divided, the weakness of the executive may require, on the other hand, that it should be fortified. An absolute negative, on the legislature, appears at first view to be the natural defence with which the executive magistrate should be armed. But perhaps it would be neither altogether safe, nor alone sufficient. On ordinary occasions, it might not be exerted with requisite firmness; and on extraordinary occasions, it might be perfidiously abused. May not this defect of an absolute negative be supplied, by some qualified connection between this weaker department, and the weaker branch of the stronger department, by which the latter may be led to support the constitutional rights of the former, without being too much detached from the rights of its own department?

If the principles on which these observations are founded be just, as I persuade myself they are, and they be applied as a criterion, to the several state constitutions, and to the federal constitution, it will be found, that if the latter does not perfectly correspond with them, the former are infinitely less able to bear such a test.

There are moreover two considerations particularly applicable to the federal system of America, which place that system in a very interesting point of view.

First. In a single republic, all the power surrendered by the people, is submitted to the administration of a single government; and usurpations are guarded against by a division of the government into distinct and separate departments. In the compound republic of America, the power surrendered by the people, is first divided between two distinct governments, and then the portion allotted to each, subdivided among distinct and separate departments. Hence a double security arises to the rights of the people. The different governments will control each other; at the same time that each will be controuled by itself.

Second. It is of great importance in a republic, not only to guard the society against the oppression of its rulers; but to guard one part of the society against the injustice of the other part. Different interests necessarily exist in different classes of citizens. If a majority be united by a common interest, the rights of the minority will be insecure. There are but two methods of providing against this evil: The one by creating a will in the community independent of the majority, that is, of the society itself; the other by comprehending in the society so many separate descriptions of citizens, as will render an unjust combination of a majority of the whole, very improbable, if not impracticable. The first method prevails in all governments possessing an hereditary or self appointed authority. This at best is but a precarious security; because a power independent of the society may as well espouse the unjust views of the major, as the rightful interests, of the minor party, and may possibly be turned against both parties. The second method will be exemplified in the federal republic of the United States. Whilst all authority in it will be derived from and dependent on the society, the society itself will be broken into so many parts, interests and classes of citizens, that the rights of individuals or of the minority, will be in little danger from interested combinations of the majority. In a free government, the security for civil rights must be the same as for religious rights. It consists in the one case in the multiplicity of interests, and in the other, in the multiplicity of sects. The degree of security in both cases will depend on the number of interests and sects; and this may be presumed to depend on the extent of country and number of people comprehended under the same government. This view of the subject must particularly recommend a proper federal system to all the sincere and considerate friends of republican government: Since it shews that in exact proportion as the territory of the union may be formed into more circumscribed confederacies or states, oppressive combinations of a majority will be facilitated, the best security under the republican form, for the rights of every class of citizens, will be diminished; and consequently, the stability and independence of some member of the government, the only other security, must be proportionally increased. Justice is the end of government. It is the end of civil society. It ever has been, and ever will be pursued, until it be obtained, or until liberty be lost in the pursuit. In a society under the forms of which the stronger faction can readily unite and oppress the weaker, anarchy may as truly be said to reign, as in a state of nature where the weaker individual is not secured against the violence of the stronger: And as in the latter state even the stronger individuals are prompted by the uncertainty of their condition, to submit to a government which may protect the weak as well as themselves: So in the former state, will the more powerful factions or parties be gradually induced by a like motive, to wish for a government which will protect all parties, the weaker as well as the more powerful. It can be little doubted, that if the state of Rhode Island was separated from the confederacy, and left to itself, the insecurity of rights under the popular form of government within such narrow limits, would be displayed by such reiterated oppressions of factious majorities, that some power altogether independent of the people would soon be called for by the voice of the very factions whose misrule had proved the necessity of it. In the extended republic of the United States, and among the great variety of interests, parties and sects which it embraces, a coalition of a majority of the whole society could seldom take place on any other principles than those of justice and the general good; and there being thus less danger to a minor from the will of the major party, there must be less pretext also, to provide for the security of the former, by introducing into the government a will not dependent on the latter; or in other words, a will independent of the society itself. It is no less certain than it is important, notwithstanding the contrary opinions which have been entertained, that the larger the society, provided it lie within a practicable sphere, the more duly capable it will be of self-government. And happily for the republican cause, the practicable sphere may be carried to a very great extent, by a judicious modification and mixture of the federal principle.

Publius [James Madison or Alexander Hamilton]

"The Federalist Number 51," [6 February] 1788. *Founders Online*. National Archives. https://founders.archives.gov/documents/Hamilton/01-04-02-0199.

Madison, James. "51 Checks and Balances." Edited by Benjamin Fletcher Wright. *The Federalist*. New York: Barnes and Noble Books, 1961.

Lesson 13

Bill of Rights, Amendments I–VIII

A bill of rights is what the people are entitled to against every government on earth, general or particular; and what no just government should refuse, or rest on inferences.
Thomas Jefferson to James Madison, 1787

Compelling Question: What were the Founders' beliefs with regard to the rights of individuals, and how did the Bill of Rights address these beliefs?

Key Concepts

1. In writing the Constitution and the Bill of Rights, the Founders protected certain rights from possible abuses by the federal government.

2. The Bill of Rights amendments clarified specific individual civil rights and set further limits to government powers beyond those already established in the Constitution.

Debate on the Bill of Rights

When the Founders wrote the Constitution, they anticipated that the new American government could abuse the rights of citizens just as Great Britain had done. They were wary of a strong central government. Therefore, the Preamble to the Constitution makes clear the intent of the new government to "secure the blessings of liberty, to ourselves and our posterity." The Framers of the Constitution remembered well that such blessings had been defined in the Declaration of Independence as the inalienable rights of "life, liberty and the pursuit of happiness."

The Constitution also protects against government abuse through separation of powers of the branches, checks and balances, and a federal system. The Founders believed that these provisions of the Constitution were sufficient to protect the natural rights of citizens.

James Madison and many other Founders, therefore, believed that a bill of rights would be unnecessary. Another reason was that bills of rights were already included in many of the state government constitutions. Those Founders who did not support a federal bill of rights thought that states were the proper level of government for protecting individual rights. Although a federal bill of rights would emphasize important rights of individuals and protections from government, it might confuse people into thinking that the list of rights was all-inclusive or that the government had more power than the Constitution had granted. These reasons convinced the Founders at the Constitutional Convention to vote unanimously against including a bill of rights in the Constitution.

During the ratification debates in the states, however, the Anti-Federalists began swaying public opinion against the Constitution. They argued that the constitutional provisions would not protect citizens' natural rights against government abuses such as those listed in the Declaration of Independence. As we saw in Session 12, the lack of a bill of rights was one reason the Anti-Federalists opposed the ratification of the Constitution.

The Federalists and Anti-Federalists finally reached a compromise. Supporters of ratification agreed to a bill of rights being added in the form of amendments to the Constitution following ratification. This pledge of a future bill of rights convinced the hesitant states to vote in favor of ratification.

James Madison, originally an opponent of a bill of rights, was the primary author of the Bill of Rights. In the First Congress, he took the lead in honoring the Federalists' pledge. He modeled the Bill of Rights after the Declaration of Rights that George Mason had written for the Virginia Constitution of 1776. In 1789, Congress accepted a conference report with proposed language for the amendments, which clarified and limited the powers of the federal government in order to safeguard the states and citizens from government abuse.

Ratification

Of the 17 amendments submitted to Congress, the senators and representatives approved 12 and sent them to President Washington, who forwarded them to the states to be ratified. Ten of the amendments were ratified by three-fourths of the states. These 10 amendments are known as the "Bill of Rights."

Following is a summary of the first eight of these amendments in the Bill of Rights and the Founders reasons for adopting them. In Session 14, we will discuss Amendments IX and X. The full text of the Bill of Rights Amendments is found at the end of this session.

Amendment I

The six rights protected in the First Amendment are all essential for a free society. They are all related and build on one another. Each of these freedoms is necessary.

When James Madison wrote, "Congress shall make no law respecting an establishment of religion," he did not intend religion to be banished from the public square. Instead, this amendment was to guard against the religious persecution and abuses citizens had experienced in England, where the government controlled the church. The Founders did not want to establish a national church, such as Great Britain and many other European nations had. They feared that a government-established church would threaten the free exercise of religion. They believed this would impede citizens from exercising their right to choose their own religion. The Founders wanted to encourage and protect churches *from* government interference. Hence, Congress cannot prohibit the free exercise of religion.

The Founders also believed that freedom of speech—even unpopular speech—is essential in a republic. Citizens must be able to freely discuss and debate issues and hold the government accountable. Freedom of speech helps society prosper through the sharing of ideas, innovation, and scientific advances. The Founders also wanted to keep government officials in check by holding them to a standard of republican principles. They believed that free speech would help ensure this accountability.

Not all speech is protected, however. The Supreme Court has restricted **slander**, speech intended to falsely damage a person's good reputation. People also have no right to make false statements that could lead to public panic.

Related to freedom of speech is freedom of the press. During the colonial period, the British government tried to censor American newspapers from publishing anti-British opinions and articles. Two Englishmen under the alias of Cato (a statesman and critic of corruption in the Roman Republic) wrote essays known as "Cato's Letters" in 1720–1723. These letters, published in newspapers in the colonies, spread revolutionary ideas. The Founders wanted to ensure that the press could criticize the new American government. **Libel**, the printed form of slander, is not protected, however.

The right of assembly provides that any group of citizens can gather together as long as their activities are peaceful and lawful. The government may limit the right of assembly only for reasons of public safety such as the size of crowds in restricted spaces or for access in case of emergencies.

Similarly, the right to petition protects the citizens' right to present grievances to the government. This right originated in the Magna Carta in 1215, which formally recognized the right of certain nobles to petition the king. Later, the British Parliament recognized the right of every subject to petition Parliament and the king. Recall from earlier sessions that the refusal of the king and Parliament to respond to colonial concerns contributed to the push for American independence. Amendment I ensures that the traditional right of citizens to make their concerns known directly to those in government will not be eroded.

Amendment II

Due to their experience with the British, the Founders were wary that the new federal government might use the military to oppress states and citizens. The right to bear arms makes sure that the American people have the right and the means to resist attempts at armed oppression by the federal government. The right to bear arms promotes two essential principles: (1) individuals have a natural right to protect and defend their property, their lives, and the lives of innocent people;

and (2) the right to bear arms allows citizens to resist government tyranny. This amendment affirms the central role citizen-soldier militias had played in winning the War of Independence. The Founders also expected that the national military policy of the United States would be founded on strong state-level militias, and such forces would require well-armed citizens.

Amendment III

This amendment protects private property from military intrusion. American colonists had experienced the abuse of their property rights after the British Parliament passed the Quartering Acts, a contributing cause of the colonies declaring independence. Before and during the Revolutionary War, British soldiers forced American homeowners to shelter and feed them. In reaction to these abuses, James Madison wrote this amendment to safeguard citizens' private property rights. In peacetime, the military is prohibited from housing its troops in private residences without the consent of the owners. In wartime, the military cannot house its troops in private residences except in accordance with established law. Thus, the amendment balances wartime needs with citizens' rights, but citizens' rights are foremost.

Amendment IV

King George's soldiers were notorious for searching colonists' homes and seizing their property without showing just cause. They violated the English principle that every person's home should be free of government intrusion unless there is reasonable suspicion of criminal activity or public danger.

Madison wrote the Fourth Amendment to prohibit the new government from committing such abuses. The amendment spells out the rights of citizens and the responsibilities of government. It prohibits unreasonable searches and seizures by government officials, usually law enforcement. The officer must obtain a warrant—with limits—to search a person's property based on "probable cause" that a crime has been committed. Requiring a warrant describing the place to be searched and good reasons for it establishes a standard for what searches the government can carry out. Officers must be accountable and follow a legal process. The Fourth Amendment is a fundamental part of criminal law in the United States.

Amendment V

Grand juries restrain government power. Because there is a danger of a judge siding with government prosecutors, a jury of peers (citizens of equal standing with the accused) convenes to ensure a fair trial. Grand juries are assembled at the direction of a prosecutor, then conduct their business in secret, and receive evidence collected by law enforcement officials. The jurors hear the evidence—without a judge—and vote either to drop the charges or proceed with criminal charges against a defendant. If criminal charges are filed, the case goes to a full trial by jury.

Grand juries protect citizens against overreach by prosecutors. These juries played an important role in guarding the colonists from charges based on unpopular British laws before the revolution, so this provision of the Bill of Rights was widely popular.

The Fifth Amendment also prohibits "double jeopardy," preventing the government from retrying a case except under the rules of **common law**.

In 1354, during the reign of King Edward III, the English Parliament adopted statutes that clarified the meaning and scope of liberties guaranteed by the Magna Carta. Included was "due process of the law," which says that a person can be judged only after first being properly notified of the charges and then appearing in court. This amendment establishes that people cannot be deprived of life, liberty, and property without due process of law. Actions against a citizen must be justified and reasonable, and appropriate legal steps must be taken. People can be charged based on laws that already exist and known by established legal procedures.

Amendment V prohibits anyone from being forced to give testimony against himself or herself in a court of law. Furthermore, it forbids the courts from treating a refusal to testify as an admission of guilt. This is the source of the famous phrase, "pleading the fifth," meaning, "I don't have to say anything against myself, and my silence doesn't mean I'm guilty."

Amendment VI

The Sixth Amendment guarantees citizens a right to a jury trial in federal courts. The right to a public trial by impartial jurors highlights the colonists' experiences with trials held in secret by the British. Secret trials allowed the government to violate rights without considering evidence of innocence.

The amendment also establishes that every accused person must be informed of the crime of which he or she has been charged and be provided with a defense attorney.

Amendment VII

This amendment established the citizen's right to a jury trial regarding property in common law cases, a right that originates in the traditional rights established in the Magna Carta.

The amendment answers the Anti-Federalist demands that a **civil jury**—not just a judge—be required under specific standards. It establishes that all citizens facing civil charges will have access to a civil jury. Just as the Founders prohibited the government from retrying criminal cases, they prohibited double jeopardy in civil cases, according to the rules of common law.

Amendment VIII

Known as the "cruel and unusual punishment amendment," the Eighth Amendment prohibits extraordinary punishments that do not fit the crime, including torture and punishments not provided by legislation.

The Founders remembered how the British would jail colonists and keep them for extended periods by not setting a reasonable **bail**. Madison wrote this amendment in reaction to abuses the colonists suffered from British officials who made the bail so high they could keep certain people in jail indefinitely.

The Supreme Court has interpreted "excessive" bail as that which is "a figure higher than reasonably calculated" (Stack v. Boyle, 1951). Because of the Eighth Amendment, a defendant can appeal a bail on the grounds of it being excessive by filing a motion for a reduced bail.

■ Key Terms

bail. An amount of money that a person accused of a crime pays to a court of law so that he or she can be released from custody until trial. The payment is a way of making certain that the person will return to court for trial.

civil jury. A group of citizens (peers) who, along with a judge, hear a complaint by a citizen or a group of citizens who claim to have suffered a wrong and seek payment or other remedy for damages. At the end of the trial, the jurors decide whether the case has merit. If the jurors believe that the person or group who brought the lawsuit is in the right, they can award compensation for injury or loss.

common law. A body of laws based on legal precedents established by the courts, as opposed to laws passed by a legislature and enacted by a federal or state executive. Also known as "case law."

grand jury. A group of citizens that examines accusations against persons charged with crimes and, if the evidence warrants, makes formal charges on which the accused persons are later tried by a judge and jury.

libel. A form of damaging someone's good reputation or character in print or through broadcast or digital media or any communication that is accessible to the public.

slander. A false and damaging oral statement about a person.

? Discussion Question

When reading the following Bill of Rights, it is important to ask how each one protects the citizen's right to life, liberty, or property. Any amendment should help to protect a citizen's basic natural rights.

Answers will vary. Students should be able to identify in each of the amendments what specifically the government is prohibited from doing. For example, "The First Amendment states that the government may not either favor or restrict any particular form of religion." Or "The Second Amendment says that it is against the law for the government to outlaw the private ownership of weapons necessary for people to defend themselves, their homes, and their communities from threats to their freedom." The Founders believed that each of the rights reflected in the Bill of Rights represented basic natural rights of citizens.

Each of these prohibitions of the authority of the government is also known as a "negative" right, meaning that the government is prohibited from infringing upon, or curtailing, the natural rights of the citizens. This is discussed specifically in Session 14.

BILL OF RIGHTS, AMENDMENTS I–X TO THE U.S. CONSTITUTION (1789)

The First Congress under the new Constitution adopted 12 articles of amendment, which President Washington sent to the states to be ratified. Three-fourths of the states ratified amendments three through 12, and they became the ten amendments to the Constitution known as the Bill of Rights.

Preamble to the 1789 Joint Resolution of the Congress Proposing 12 Amendments to the U.S. Constitution

The Conventions of a number of the States, having at the time of their adopting the Constitution, expressed a desire, in order to prevent misconstruction or abuse of its powers, that further declaratory and restrictive clauses should be added: And as extending the ground of public confidence in the Government, will best ensure the beneficent ends of its institution.

Ratified by the States December 15, 1791

Amendment I

Congress shall make no law respecting an establishment of religion, or prohibiting the free exercise thereof; or abridging the freedom of speech, or of the press; or the right of the people peaceably to assemble, and to petition the Government for a redress of grievances.

Amendment II

A well regulated Militia, being necessary to the security of a free State, the right of the people to keep and bear Arms, shall not be infringed.

Amendment III

No Soldier shall, in time of peace be quartered in any house, without the consent of the Owner, nor in time of war, but in a manner to be prescribed by law.

Amendment IV

The right of the people to be secure in their persons, houses, papers, and effects, against unreasonable searches and seizures, shall not be violated, and no Warrants shall issue, but upon probable cause, supported by Oath or affirmation, and particularly describing the place to be searched, and the persons or things to be seized.

Amendment V

No person shall be held to answer for a capital, or otherwise infamous crime, unless on a presentment or indictment of a Grand Jury, except in cases arising in the land or naval forces, or in the Militia, when in actual service in time of War or public danger; nor shall any person be subject for the same offence to be twice put in jeopardy of life or limb; nor shall be compelled in any criminal case to be a witness against himself, nor be deprived of life, liberty, or property, without due process of law; nor shall private property be taken for public use, without just compensation.

Amendment VI

In all criminal prosecutions, the accused shall enjoy the right to a speedy and public trial, by an impartial jury of the State and district wherein the crime shall have been committed, which district shall have been previously ascertained by law, and to be informed of the nature and cause of the accusation; to be confronted with the witnesses against him; to have compulsory process for obtaining witnesses in his favor, and to have the Assistance of Counsel for his defence.

Amendment VII

In Suits at common law, where the value in controversy shall exceed twenty dollars, the right of trial by jury shall be preserved, and no fact tried by a jury, shall be otherwise re-examined in any Court of the United States, than according to the rules of the common law.

Amendment VIII

Excessive bail shall not be required, nor excessive fines imposed, nor cruel and unusual punishments inflicted.

Amendment IX

The enumeration in the Constitution, of certain rights, shall not be construed to deny or disparage others retained by the people.

Amendment X

The powers not delegated to the United States by the Constitution, nor prohibited by it to the States, are reserved to the States respectively, or to the people.

Lesson 14

Bill of Rights, Amendments IX and X and Federalism

The powers delegated by the proposed Constitution to the Federal Government are few and defined. Those which are to remain in the State Governments are numerous and indefinite. The former will be exercised principally on external objects, as war, peace, negotiation, and foreign commerce; . . . The powers reserved to the states will extend to all the objects, which, in the ordinary course of affairs, concern the lives, liberties and properties of the people, and the internal order, improvement, and prosperity of the state.

James Madison, The Federalist No. 45

Compelling Question: How do Amendments IX and X protect individual rights from encroachment by the federal government?

Key Concepts

1. The Bill of Rights is not a full enumeration of the rights that Americans possess. This is made clear in the Ninth Amendment.

2. The Tenth Amendment guarantees that the powers not specifically listed in the Constitution or Bill of Rights are retained by the states or the people. The amendment also affirms the vital structural role that states play in the American government.

3. Federalism promotes a strong federal government that is able to defend the nation while enabling the states to deal with the issues concerning the people of their states. But another aspect of federalism is that it allows a healthy check on government power—decentralizing it and balancing power between the states and federal government.

What Makes Amendments IX and X Different?

As discussed in Session 13, the first eight amendments to the Constitution in the Bill of Rights all share one common characteristic: they all *prohibit* the federal government from infringing on certain *specific* rights enjoyed by individuals. Each amendment includes the same basic three components, stating:

- Why a particular right is important;
- What the specific right is; and
- What the federal government is prohibited from doing that would compromise that particular right.

Amendment II illustrates these three parts:
- A well-regulated Militia, being necessary to the security of a free State
- The right of the people to keep and bear Arms
- Shall not be infringed.

The first eight amendments do not necessarily list the three parts in the same order. But each amendment does identify a specific "negative" right and states that the federal government is not allowed to infringe on *that* particular right. But do these eight amendments lead to the conclusion that any rights *not* addressed in the Constitution are automatically subject to federal authority?

Amendment IX

During the drafting of the Bill of Rights, some Founders questioned whether people might think that no rights existed other than those included in the Bill of Rights. The Anti-Federalists wanted the Constitution to be clear and unmistakable regarding what rights the new federal government was prohibited from restricting. At the same time, they did not want to assume that the new federal government automatically had the authority to restrict any rights that the people recognized and enjoyed but that were not specifically listed in the Constitution. Simply put, the Ninth Amendment provides that the rights **enumerated** here are not to be understood as *all* the rights that exist.

The Federalists, including Alexander Hamilton and James Madison, originally thought it unnecessary to add anything more to the Constitution on this issue. In *Federalist No. 84*, Hamilton writes, "Why declare that things shall not be done which there is no power to do?" But the Anti-Federalists feared that the federal government could expand its powers and limit the rights of citizens.

As discussed in Session 13, the Federalists agreed to present a bill of rights in the form of amendments to encourage states to ratify the Constitution. Madison, in fact, became convinced of the importance of allaying people's fears that the federal government could encroach on their liberties. In his speech introducing the Bill of Rights on June 8, 1789, Madison refers to the need for the Ninth Amendment: "It is true the powers of the general government are **circumscribed** [not bold in original]; they are directed to particular objects; but even if government keeps within those limits, it has certain discretionary powers with respect to the means, which may admit of abuse." He goes on to say that the Ninth Amendment addresses all the other individual rights not "thrown into the hands of the government." To that end, Amendment IX reads: "The enumeration in the Constitution, of certain rights, shall not be construed to deny or disparage others retained by the people."

As with the other amendments, Amendment IX is a **negative right**—it prohibits the federal government from infringing upon any rights of the people, even if such rights are not specifically enumerated.

Government in the United States of America is based on the consent of the governed because all people have **inalienable** rights, and all are equal as human beings. The Ninth Amendment confirms that people retain these rights and that the list of rights in the Bill of Rights is not complete. It is a partial list. The government is not to **disparage** rights not listed in the Constitution, and the only powers the federal and state governments have are those **delegated** by the people. The enumerated powers in the Constitution protect the rights of the people and were intended to be limited. However, definitions have changed, and the role and scope of federal power have expanded greatly over the last century. (See "Modern Interpretation of 'Promote the General Welfare'" in Session 8.)

Amendment X

Like other amendments in the Bill of Rights, the Tenth Amendment was proposed to satisfy the demands of the Anti-Federalists for protection against a stronger federal government under the Constitution than under the Articles of Confederation. In fact, the Tenth Amendment is similar to Article II of the Articles of Confederation, which reads: The powers not delegated to the United States by the Constitution, nor prohibited by it to the States, are reserved to the States respectively, or to the people.

Amendment X is unique within the Bill of Rights. It is the only one of the ten amendments that doesn't explicitly affirm a negative right, which means that the federal government must not infringe on a specific stated right belonging to the people or states. However, Amendment X works in partnership with Amendment IX to affirm that any rights or authorities that the Constitution doesn't specifically assign to the federal government are understood to belong to the states or the citizens.

The Tenth Amendment affirms the principle of federalism that the powers of the federal government are only those delegated to it by the people and granted in the Constitution. The system of federalism divides power between the federal government and the states. The amendment clarifies the relationship between the federal government and the Bill of Rights, as well as between the federal government and the states. This restricts the government and protects liberty. The people in the states possess all powers not explicitly given to the federal government.

States' Rights is a common expression referring to any rights that are not addressed under the Constitution and that are therefore within the scope of the states to protect. However, it is important to keep in mind that the Constitution does *not* recognize any level of government as having rights in the same sense that individual people have rights. The Constitution allocates the authority to perform specific actions and responsibilities on behalf of the citizens of the United States and empowers the government to the extent necessary to fulfill those responsibilities.

Federalism

The principle of federalism employed by the Founders was key to the creation of the United States. The Thirteen Colonies had developed their governments, and they would not unite under a federal government unless they could retain elements of sovereignty. Federalism—the division of power between the states and the national government—is an essential part of the United States of America. The Constitution created an effective yet limited government that would secure the natural rights of citizens while respecting the power of the states. Certain powers are delegated to the federal government, but all other powers are retained by the states or the people. States can regulate the behavior of their citizens and pass laws that represent the local interests of their citizens as long as the laws do not violate the U.S. Constitution.

Federalism protects the liberty of all citizens against a centralized national government by maintaining the vitality of strong state governments that can check federal overreach. Federalism protects the states from being absolutely controlled by the federal government and allows for citizens in one state to pass laws based on values not shared in other states. It ensures the decentralization of authority and promotes local self-government, liberty, and civic virtue.

Modern Examples of Federalism Guaranteed by Amendments IX and X

Throughout much of United States history, Amendment IX went unchallenged and was often overlooked. Were Madison, Hamilton, and Jay correct when they argued in *The Federalist* that a specific protection of any unenumerated rights wasn't necessary? It was not until 1965 that the Supreme Court issued a ruling (*Griswold v. Connecticut*) that relied explicitly on Amendment IX. The Court determined that individuals enjoy a constitutionally protected right to privacy with regard to the use of birth control. In support of the court's decision, the justices said:

> To hold that a right so basic and fundamental and so deep-rooted in our society as the right of privacy in marriage may be infringed because that right is not guaranteed in so many words by the first eight amendments to the Constitution is to ignore the Ninth Amendment and to give it no effect whatsoever.

Despite dissent on the court regarding the undeniable truth that a "right to privacy" is nowhere enumerated in the Constitution, seven of the nine Supreme Court justices agreed that such a right is addressed under the authority of Amendment IX.

Likewise, since its ratification in 1791, Amendment X was often overlooked or dismissed by legal scholars as simply reaffirming what the Federalists had argued prior to ratification of the Constitution. However, late in the twentieth century, states began to take advantage of the protections of Amendment X. In the 1992 case of *New York v. United States,* the Supreme Court ruled that the State of New York could not be forced to comply with federal regulations regarding handling hazardous waste. In this case, the justices cited the Tenth Amendment, saying:

> States are not mere political subdivisions of the United States. State governments are neither regional offices nor administrative agencies of the Federal Government. The positions occupied by state officials appear nowhere on the Federal Government's most detailed organizational chart.

Amendment X was the authority by which the federal government was prohibited from compelling the State of New York to accept ownership of toxic waste simply by directing it do so.

These examples illustrate how even amendments that seemed unnecessary when they were adopted turned out to be necessary and vital. Although it took nearly two hundred years after ratification and reflected circumstances the Founders could never have imagined, all ten of the amendments in the Bill of Rights have been validated as foundational to protecting the framework of federalism established in the Constitution.

■ Key Terms

circumscribe. To limit or restrict.

delegate. To entrust authority or responsibility to act from one person or agency to another.

disparage. To regard as having little worth; undervalue.

enumerate. To list separately.

federalism. A political system in which states unite to create a national government while retaining many of their powers; the division of power between states and the federal government.

inalienable. Referring to certain universal rights recognized by the Declaration of Independence and the U.S. Constitution that cannot be taken away or given away by government because they are naturally given to all individuals by their Creator at birth and are retained throughout life. (In law, a "lien" is a claim on the property of another.)

negative right. A right that a government, group, or person must not infringe on or prohibit; freedom from some action imposed by a government, group, or person.

states' rights. The powers that the U.S. Constitution does not delegate to the federal government nor prohibit the states from exercising.

? Discussion Questions

1. What does the Ninth Amendment protect?

   The Bill of Rights is not a complete list of all the rights that citizens possess. Therefore, the Ninth Amendment was written to protect the rights not included in the Bill of Rights.

2. What does the Tenth Amendment protect?

   The Tenth Amendment protects the rights of the states and of the people to possess the powers that the Constitution does not grant to the federal government.

3. What is federalism and why is it important?

   Federalism refers to the division of government power between the local, state, and federal governments. This division limits the power of government and protects liberty by involving more citizens and decentralizing power to encourage local self-government.

   The Constitution was intended to create an effective yet limited national government that would secure the natural rights of citizens. It does so by granting those powers needed for important national functions to the federal government while leaving all other powers to the states or the people. Federalism protects the liberty of the citizens against a centralized government by maintaining the vitality of strong state governments able to check federal overreach. Federalism protects the states from being overwhelmed by the national government, allowing for the decentralization of authority and promoting local self-government, liberty, and civic virtue.

4. Does federalism mean that states have rights?

   Although the Tenth Amendment is referred to as the "States' Rights Amendment," states themselves do not have any rights. Only people have rights. But the powers not granted to the federal government in the Constitution are reserved to states and individuals. Ultimately, the federal and state governments are created by and serve the people and have whatever powers the people choose to give them through the U.S. Constitution and state constitutions.

   Article VI states that the Constitution "shall be the supreme Law of the Land." The Constitution supersedes all laws passed by lower-level governments. Federal laws and treaties also must not conflict with the Constitution. The Constitution's hierarchy of supremacy seeks to prevent government abuses of power because it enumerates our rights and does not let government operate on the whims of those in power.

Lesson 15

Amendments XI–XVII

The Congress, whenever two thirds of both Houses shall deem it necessary, shall propose Amendments to this Constitution, or, on the Application of the Legislatures of two thirds of the several States, shall call a Convention for proposing Amendments.

U.S. Constitution, Article V

Compelling Question: How does each amendment either increase or decrease individual rights and freedoms, or how do they expand or limit the power of the federal government?

Key Concepts

1. After the Bill of Rights was ratified in 1791, seventeen more amendments were adopted over time based on social changes and historical trends.

2. Some of the amendments increased individual rights and freedoms. Other amendments increased the power of the federal government at the expense of individual rights and freedoms.

3. The Founders knew there would be changes in society that would require changes to our laws. They established two ways to correct injustices, by passing new laws and by amending the Constitution.

Amendment XI – Authority of Federal Courts Restricted; Principle of State Sovereign Immunity Established

The Judicial power of the United States shall not be construed to extend to any suit in law or equity, commenced or prosecuted against one of the United States by Citizens of another State, or by Citizens or Subjects of any Foreign State.

Effect: Ratified in 1795, the 11th Amendment to the U.S. Constitution, says that federal courts cannot hear cases and make decisions against a state if it is sued by a citizen who lives in another state or a person who lives in another country. In other words, it establishes the principle that states have immunity against lawsuits by citizens of another state or country in federal court.

Amendment XII – Electoral College Process for Electing the President and Vice President Changed

The Electors shall meet in their respective states, and vote by ballot for President and Vice-President, one of whom, at least, shall not be an inhabitant of the same state with themselves; they shall name in their ballots the person voted for as President, and in distinct ballots the person voted for as Vice-President, and they shall make distinct lists of all persons voted for as President, and all persons voted for as Vice-President and of the number of votes for each, which lists they shall sign and certify, and transmit sealed to the seat of the government of the United States, directed to the President of the Senate;—The President of the Senate shall, in the presence of the Senate and House of Representatives, open all the certificates and the votes shall then be counted;—The person having the greatest number of votes for President, shall be the President, if such number be a majority of the whole number of Electors appointed; and if no person have such majority, then from the persons having the highest numbers not exceeding three on the list of those voted for as President, the House of Representatives shall choose immediately, by ballot, the President. But in choosing the President, the votes shall be taken by states, the representation from each state having one vote; a quorum for this purpose shall consist of a member or members from two-thirds of the states, and a majority of all the states shall be necessary to a choice. [And if the House of Representatives shall not choose a President whenever the right of choice shall devolve upon them, before the fourth day of March next following, then the Vice-President shall act as President, as in the case of the death or other constitutional disability of the President.—*The person having the greatest number of votes as Vice-President, shall be the Vice-President, if such number be a majority of the whole number of Electors appointed, and if no person have a majority, then from the two highest numbers on the list, the Senate shall choose the Vice-President; a quorum for the purpose shall consist of two-thirds of the whole number of Senators, and a majority of the whole number shall be necessary to a choice. But no person constitutionally ineligible to the office of President shall be eligible to that of Vice-President of the United States.*

*This provision was superseded by Sections 1 and 3 of the 20th Amendment in 1933.

Effect: Passed by Congress in 1803 and ratified in 1804, the 12th Amendment provides for separate **Electoral College** votes for President and Vice President, correcting weaknesses in the earlier electoral system that were responsible for the controversial Presidential Election of 1800.

Changing the Constitution regarding Slavery and Inequality

The scourge of slavery in America continued long after the Declaration of Independence and ratification of the U.S. Constitution and Bill of Rights. While support for slavery declined in the North over time, the demand for slave labor in the South increased exponentially with the invention of the cotton gin, patented in 1794. Beginning in the 1830s, many former slaves and abolitionists spoke out against slavery in public debates and published tracts and newspaper articles. Eventually, the heroic efforts of African American and white abolitionists led to a change in American culture. A consensus developed in the northern states that slavery must be abolished.

Abolitionists were outraged by the U.S. Supreme Court's Dred Scott decision of 1857, which ruled that Dred Scott was not a U.S. citizen because he was a descendant of African American slaves and that slave owners could transport their slaves to the territories. The decision essentially made slavery legal in the "free" territories and denied constitutional rights of citizenship to African Americans, both free and enslaved. It also stopped debate and compromise in Congress on the issue of slavery because the ruling said that Congress could no longer make laws regarding the legality of slavery in the territories.

The Dred Scott decision led to a further divide between the North and South over slavery and culminated in the secession of southern states from the Union and the creation of the Confederate States of America. President Lincoln, by executive order, issued the Emancipation Proclamation of September 22, 1862, to free enslaved people living in the Confederacy as of January 1, 1863. But the Civil War raged on, devastating the country and resulting in more than 600,000 deaths. After the Union won, Congress passed the 13th Amendment to finally abolish slavery in the United States. It was ratified in 1865. In 1868, the Dred Scott decision was overturned by the ratification of the 13th Amendment, which outlawed slavery, and the 14th Amendment, which granted former slaves the right of citizenship by birth or naturalization and equal protection of the laws.

After much struggle, voting rights for citizens of all races and for women were granted by ratification of the 15th and 19th Amendments (Session 16). And the voting age was lowered to 18 years by the 26th Amendment (Session 16).

Amendment XIII – Slavery Outlawed

Section 1. *Neither slavery nor involuntary servitude, except as a punishment for crime whereof the party shall have been duly convicted, shall exist within the United States, or any place subject to their jurisdiction.* ***Section 2.*** *Congress shall have power to enforce this article by appropriate legislation.*

Effect: The Civil War between the United States and the Confederate States that seceded from the Union was primarily fought because of the evil of slavery. More than 600,000 men and women lost their lives. As a result, Amendment XIII was ratified in 1865, outlawing slavery and involuntary servitude—except when applied as punishment for a crime—in the entire United States.

Amendment XIV – Citizenship by Birth or Naturalization in U.S. and Equal Protection under the Law Granted to All, Including Former Slaves

Section 1. *All persons born or naturalized in the United States, and subject to the jurisdiction thereof, are citizens of the United States and of the State wherein they reside. No State shall make or enforce any law which shall abridge the privileges or immunities of citizens of the United States; nor shall any State deprive any person of life, liberty, or property, without due process of law; nor deny to any person within its jurisdiction the equal protection of the laws.*

Section 2. *Representatives shall be apportioned among the several States according to their respective numbers, counting the whole number of persons in each State, excluding Indians not taxed. But when the right to vote at any election for the choice of electors for President and Vice-*

President of the United States, Representatives in Congress, the Executive and Judicial officers of a State, or the members of the Legislature thereof, is denied to any of the male inhabitants of such State, being twenty-one years of age,* and citizens of the United States, or in any way abridged, except for participation in rebellion, or other crime, the basis of representation therein shall be reduced in the proportion which the number of such male citizens shall bear to the whole number of male citizens twenty-one years of age in such State.

Section 3. *No person shall be a Senator or Representative in Congress, or elector of President and Vice-President, or hold any office, civil or military, under the United States, or under any State, who, having previously taken an oath, as a member of Congress, or as an officer of the United States, or as a member of any State legislature, or as an executive or judicial officer of any State, to support the Constitution of the United States, shall have engaged in insurrection or rebellion against the same, or given aid or comfort to the enemies thereof. But Congress may by a vote of two-thirds of each House, remove such disability.*

Section 4. *The validity of the public debt of the United States, authorized by law, including debts incurred for payment of pensions and bounties for services in suppressing insurrection or rebellion, shall not be questioned. But neither the United States nor any State shall assume or pay any debt or obligation incurred in aid of insurrection or rebellion against the United States, or any claim for the loss or emancipation of any slave; but all such debts, obligations, and claims shall be held illegal and void.*

Section 5. *The Congress shall have the power to enforce, by appropriate legislation, the provisions of this article.*

*Changed by Section 1 of the 26th Amendment.

Effect: The 14th Amendment to the U.S. Constitution, ratified in 1868, granted citizenship to all persons born or **naturalized** in the United States—including former slaves—and guaranteed all citizens "equal protection of the laws." Therefore, it overturned the Dred Scott Supreme Court decision. It was one of three amendments ratified during the **Reconstruction** era to abolish slavery and establish civil rights for black Americans. Over the years, the amendment would become the basis for many landmark Supreme Court decisions.

Amendment XV – Voting Rights for All Races Guaranteed

Section 1. *The right of citizens of the United States to vote shall not be denied or abridged by the United States or by any State on account of race, color, or previous condition of servitude.*

Section 2. *The Congress shall have power to enforce this article by appropriate legislation.*

Effect: The 15th Amendment, the third amendment of the Reconstruction era, granted African American men the right to vote. It was ratified into the U.S. Constitution in 1870. Despite the amendment, by the late 1870s discriminatory practices were used to prevent blacks from exercising their right to vote, an example of racism that led to passage of the Civil Rights Act of 1964 and efforts to improve race relations in America's search for a more perfect union.

Amendment XVI – Federal Income Taxes Authorized

The Congress shall have power to lay and collect taxes on incomes, from whatever source derived, without apportionment among the several States, and without regard to any census or enumeration.

Effect: Ratified in 1913, the 16th Amendment allows the federal government to levy (collect) an income tax from all Americans. Recall that this is a significant change from the original structure of the Constitution, which had previously placed strict limits on how the federal government could raise revenue. Income taxes allow for the federal government to directly tax individuals based on their personal earnings rather than in indirect ways, such as tariffs and fees on goods and services. Taxing individuals provides for a much larger revenue base for raising funds than previous methods. One of the effects has been to increase the power of the federal government at the expense of the states. The 16th Amendment has allowed the size, scope, and power of the federal government to grow dramatically larger than the Founders originally envisioned.

Amendment XVII – U.S. Senators Elected by Popular Vote instead of by State Legislatures

The Senate of the United States shall be composed of two Senators from each State, elected by the people thereof, for six years; and each Senator shall have one vote. The electors in each State shall have the qualifications requisite for electors of the most numerous branch of the State legislatures. When vacancies happen in the representation of any State in the Senate, the executive authority of such State shall issue writs of election to fill such vacancies: Provided, That the legislature of any State may empower the executive thereof to make temporary appointments until the people fill the vacancies by election as the legislature may direct. This amendment shall not be so construed as to affect the election or term of any Senator chosen before it becomes valid as part of the Constitution.

Effect: Ratified by the states in 1913, the 17th Amendment modified Article I, Section 3, of the Constitution by allowing voters to cast direct votes for U.S. senators. Prior to its passage, senators were chosen by state legislatures. This change resulted in less power of the states.

■ Key Terms

abolitionist. A person who sought to abolish or outlaw slavery, especially in the period leading up to and during the U.S. Civil War.

Electoral College. A body of people, called "electors," who represent the states of the U.S. and who formally cast votes for the election of the president and vice president.

naturalized citizen. A person who is not a citizen by birth in the United States but who has been granted citizenship after he or she fulfills the requirements established by Congress in the Immigration and Nationality Act.

tariff. A fee or charge added to the price of imported goods, such as fruits or vegetables grown overseas, when brought into the country to be sold. Tariffs on international goods were originally the principal means of funding the U.S. federal government.

Discussion Questions

1. Which amendments changed *how* the federal government functions? (Changes to rules such as how officials are elected, appointed, or removed from office)

   Amendment XII changed how the president and vice president were chosen by the Electoral College to ensure that both positions were filled as a unified ticket. Amendment XVII changed the method of electing senators, requiring states to use a system of direct popular voting.

2. Which amendments **increased** individual rights of citizenship? (Changes that expanded citizenship and voting access)

   Amendment XIII abolished slavery. Amendment XIV extended citizenship to all former slaves and ensured citizenship for all individuals born within the sovereign territory of the United States. Amendment XV extended voting rights to former slaves. Some consider Amendment XVII to have strengthened voting rights of individuals by requiring the direct election of senators.

3. Which amendments **increased** the power of the federal government (Changes that expanded federal authority, taxation, or representation at the expense of the states or individuals)

   Amendment XVI provided for direct taxation of U.S. citizens in the form of a tax on income. By requiring the direct election of U.S. senators, Amendment XVII also strengthened the federal government and weakened the power of the individual states.

4. Which amendments **decreased** the power of the federal government? (Changes that restricted federal authority, taxation, or representation to the benefit of the states or individuals)

   Amendment XI restricted the scope of federal courts from judging a case against a state brought by an individual who is not a resident of that state or who lives in a foreign country.

Lesson 16

Amendments XVIII–XXVII

Today's Constitution is a realistic document of freedom only because of several corrective amendments. Those amendments speak to a sense of decency and fairness that I and other Blacks cherish.

Thurgood Marshall, *the first African American Justice of the Supreme Court of the United States*

Compelling Question: How does each amendment either increase or decrease individual rights and freedoms, or how do they expand or limit the power of the federal government?

Key Concepts

1. After the Bill of Rights was ratified in 1791, seventeen more amendments were adopted over time based on social changes, correcting injustices, and historical trends. This session examines Amendments XVIII–XXVII.

2. Some of the amendments increased individual rights and freedoms. Other amendments increased the power of the federal government at the expense of the states or individual rights and freedoms.

Amendment XVIII – Liquor Outlawed (Prohibition)

Section 1. After one year from the ratification of this article the manufacture, sale, or transportation of intoxicating liquors within, the importation thereof into, or the exportation thereof from the United States and all territory subject to the jurisdiction thereof for beverage purposes is hereby prohibited.

Section 2. The Congress and the several States shall have concurrent power to enforce this article by appropriate legislation.

Section 3. This article shall be inoperative unless it shall have been ratified as an amendment to the Constitution by the legislatures of the several States, as provided in the Constitution, within seven years from the date of the submission hereof to the States by the Congress.

Effect: By the late 1800s, **prohibition** movements had sprung up across the United States, driven by social and religious groups that considered abuse of alcohol, specifically drunkenness, a threat to the nation. Ratified in 1919, the 18th Amendment declared the production, transport, and sale of intoxicating liquors illegal, though it did not outlaw the actual consumption of alcohol. Shortly after the amendment was ratified, Congress passed the Volstead Act to provide for the federal enforcement of Prohibition. However, Prohibition did not stop the production and distribution of alcoholic beverages, so consumption of alcohol continued via establishments that operated quietly and "under the radar."

Amendment XIX – Voting Rights for Men and Women (Women's Suffrage) Granted

The right of citizens of the United States to vote shall not be denied or abridged by the United States or by any State on account of sex. Congress shall have power to enforce this article by appropriate legislation.

Effect: Ratified in 1920, the 19th Amendment to the U.S. Constitution granted American women the right to vote, a right known as "women's **suffrage**." It ended a century of protest and helped millions of women move closer to equality in American life.

Amendment XX – Start and End Dates for Terms of the President and Congress Established

Section 1. The terms of the President and Vice President shall end at noon on the 20th day of January, and the terms of Senators and Representatives at noon on the 3d day of January, of the years in which such terms would have ended if this article had not been ratified; and the terms of their successors shall then begin.

Section 2. The Congress shall assemble at least once in every year, and such meeting shall begin at noon on the 3d day of January, unless they shall by law appoint a different day.

Section 3. If, at the time fixed for the beginning of the term of the President, the President elect shall have died, the Vice President elect shall become President. If a President shall not have been chosen before the time fixed for the beginning of his term, or if the President elect shall have failed to qualify, then the Vice President elect shall act as President until a President shall have qualified; and the Congress may by law provide for the case wherein neither a President elect nor a Vice President elect shall have qualified, declaring who shall then act as President, or the manner in which one who is to act shall be selected, and such person shall act accordingly until a President or Vice President shall have qualified.

Section 4. *The Congress may by law provide for the case of the death of any of the persons from whom the House of Representatives may choose a President whenever the right of choice shall have devolved upon them, and for the case of the death of any of the persons from whom the Senate may choose a Vice President whenever the right of choice shall have devolved upon them.*

Section 5. *Sections 1 and 2 shall take effect on the 15th day of October following the ratification of this article.*

Section 6. *This article shall be inoperative unless it shall have been ratified as an amendment to the Constitution by the legislatures of three-fourths of the several States within seven years from the date of its submission.*

Effect: The 20th Amendment, ratified in 1933, was designed to shorten the "lame duck" period served by members of Congress and the president after an election but before the end of the terms of those who were not reelected. Most important was that it ended long sessions of Congress beginning in December of odd-numbered years and short lame duck sessions in December to March of even-numbered years. The amendment established that Congress would begin every year on January 3, and the incoming president and vice president would be inaugurated on January 20 rather than on March 4. The new congressional start date was chosen so that the incoming Congress would vote in case of an Electoral College deadlock. Finally, the amendment provided for the vice president to become president if the president died. (See the 25th Amendment for more detail on presidential and vice-presidential succession.)

Amendment XXI – Control of Liquor Returned to the States (Repeal of Prohibition)

Section 1. *The eighteenth article of amendment to the Constitution of the United States is hereby repealed.*

Section 2. *The transportation or importation into any State, Territory, or Possession of the United States for delivery or use therein of intoxicating liquors, in violation of the laws thereof, is hereby prohibited.*

Section 3. *This article shall be inoperative unless it shall have been ratified as an amendment to the Constitution by conventions in the several States, as provided in the Constitution, within seven years from the date of the submission hereof to the States by the Congress.*

Effect: The 18th Amendment's prohibition of the "manufacture, sale, or transportation of intoxicating liquors" did reduce its consumption, but it forced purchases onto the **"black market."** Organized crime grew, and Prohibition was impossible to enforce. Public disillusionment led Congress to pass the 21st Amendment, which was ratified in 1933. This amendment repealed Prohibition (imposed fourteen years earlier).

Amendment XXII – Presidents Limited to Two Terms in Office

Section 1. *No person shall be elected to the office of the President more than twice, and no person who has held the office of President, or acted as President, for more than two years of a term to which some other person was elected President shall be elected to the office of the President more than once. But this article shall not apply to any person holding the office of President when this article was proposed by the Congress, and shall not prevent any person who may be holding the office of President, or acting as President, during the term within which this article becomes operative from holding the office of President or acting as President during the remainder of such term.*

Section 2. *This article shall be inoperative unless it shall have been ratified as an amendment to the Constitution by the legislatures of three-fourths of the several states within seven years from the date of its submission to the states by the Congress.*

Effect: The 22nd Amendment was advocated by those who thought that President Franklin Roosevelt's three consecutive terms were excessive. He had been reelected to a fourth term and died in the first year of the fourth term. The amendment was ratified by the states in 1951. It limits any president to two elected terms. Proponents argued that the amendment was needed to ratify a well established American tradition, begun by George Washington, that a president should step away from his duties after serving eight years.

The only extension allowed is for a vice president who fills out a presidential term and then wins two election victories.

Amendment XXIII – Presidential Electors Granted to the District of Columbia

Section 1. *The District constituting the seat of government of the United States shall appoint in such manner as the Congress may direct: A number of electors of President and Vice President equal to the whole number of Senators and Representatives in Congress to which the District would be entitled if it were a state, but in no event more than the least populous state; they shall be in addition to those appointed by the states, but they shall be considered, for the purposes of the election of President and Vice President, to be electors appointed by a state; and they shall meet in the District and perform such duties as provided by the twelfth article of amendment.*

Section 2. *The Congress shall have power to enforce this article by appropriate legislation.*

Effect: The Founders established the District of Columbia in 1791 as the capital of the United States. They named it after George Washington to honor him. Yet, since it was the seat of national government and not a state, they did not allow those living in Washington, D.C., to vote in national elections. The 23rd Amendment, ratified in 1961, declared that the District of Columbia would receive as many electoral college votes for President and Vice President as "the whole number of Senators and Representatives in Congress to which the District would be entitled if it were a state, but in no event more than the least populous state." In practice, this means that Washington, D.C., is allotted three electors.

Amendment XXIV – Voting Rights Protected; Poll Taxes Prohibited

Section 1. *The right of citizens of the United States to vote in any primary or other election for President or Vice President, for electors for President or Vice President, or for Senator or Representative in Congress, shall not be denied or abridged by the United States or any state by reason of failure to pay any poll tax or other tax.*

Section 2. *The Congress shall have power to enforce this article by appropriate legislation.*

Effect: Not long ago, citizens in some states had to pay a fee to vote in a national election. This fee was called a "poll tax." In 1964, the United States ratified the 24th Amendment to prohibit any poll tax in elections for federal officials. This removed a barrier that had prevented many low-income citizens from voting.

Amendment XXV – Process for Replacing the President and Vice President Established

Section 1. In case of the removal of the President from office or of his death or resignation, the Vice President shall become President.

Section 2. Whenever there is a vacancy in the office of the Vice President, the President shall nominate a Vice President who shall take office upon confirmation by a majority vote of both Houses of Congress.

Section 3. Whenever the President transmits to the President pro tempore of the Senate and the Speaker of the House of Representatives his written declaration that he is unable to discharge the powers and duties of his office, and until he transmits to them a written declaration to the contrary, such powers and duties shall be discharged by the Vice President as Acting President.

Section 4. Whenever the Vice President and a majority of either the principal officers of the executive departments or of such other body as Congress may by law provide, transmit to the President pro tempore of the Senate and the Speaker of the House of Representatives their written declaration that the President is unable to discharge the powers and duties of his office, the Vice President shall immediately assume the powers and duties of the office as Acting President. Thereafter, when the President transmits to the President pro tempore of the Senate and the Speaker of the House of Representatives his written declaration that no inability exists, he shall resume the powers and duties of his office unless the Vice President and a majority of either the principal officers of the executive department or of such other body as Congress may by law provide, transmit within four days to the President pro tempore of the Senate and the Speaker of the House of Representatives their written declaration that the President is unable to discharge the powers and duties of his office. Thereupon Congress shall decide the issue, assembling within forty-eight hours for that purpose if not in session. If the Congress, within twenty-one days after receipt of the latter written declaration, or, if Congress is not in session, within twenty-one days after Congress is required to assemble, determines by two-thirds vote of both Houses that the President is unable to discharge the powers and duties of his office, the Vice President shall continue to discharge the same as Acting President; otherwise, the President shall resume the powers and duties of his office.

Effect: The 25th Amendment, ratified by the states in 1967 in the aftermath of the assassination of President John F. Kennedy, provides the procedures for replacing the president or vice president in the event of death, removal, resignation, or incapacitation. These procedures were first applied in the 1970s when Gerald Ford replaced Spiro Agnew as vice president, next when Ford replaced Richard Nixon as president, and then when Nelson Rockefeller filled the resulting vacancy to become vice president.

Amendment XXVI – Voting Rights Granted for All Citizens Eighteen or Older

Section 1. The right of citizens of the United States, who are eighteen years of age or older, to vote, shall not be denied or abridged by the United States or any state on account of age.

Section 2. The Congress shall have the power to enforce this article by appropriate legislation.

Effect: In 1971, the 26th Amendment to the Constitution took effect, lowering the universal voting age in America from 21 years to 18 years. The rationale was that many 18-year-olds were fighting (and some dying) for their country during Vietnam War military service. Millions of young Americans were extended the right to vote, empowering more young people than ever before to help shape our country.

Amendment XXVII – Salary Changes of U.S. Senators and Representatives Delayed until the Next Term

No law, varying the compensation for the services of the Senators and Representatives, shall take effect, until an election of Representatives shall have intervened.

Effect: Originally proposed by the First Congress as one of twelve amendments sent to the states, this amendment was not ratified until 1992. It prohibits Congress from passing raises for themselves. Legislation that increases or decreases the salaries of members of Congress cannot take effect until the start of the next set of terms for senators and representatives.

Key Terms

black market. An illegal traffic or trade in officially controlled or scarce commodities.

prohibition. (often capitalized) The act or practice of forbidding something by law; referring to prohibiting the manufacture, sale, and transportation of alcoholic beverages.

suffrage. The right to vote in political elections.

Discussion Questions

1. Which amendments in this session changed the rules related to federal terms of office, replacement of the president or vice president, or removal from office?

   Amendment XX changed the dates of inauguration of the newly elected president and vice president, from March to January, following the prior November election. Amendment XXII imposed a two-term limit on the office of the president. Amendment XXV provides a means for removal of the president in the event of physical or mental incapacitation, and the smooth transition of power to the vice president. Amendment XXVII provides for a delay in changes of salaries to members of Congress so that they go into effect after the current congressional term.

2. Which amendments **increased** individual rights of citizenship? (Changes that expanded citizenship and voting access)

   Amendment XIX extended voting rights to women. Amendment XXIII extended presidential electoral rights to residents of the District of Columbia. Amendment XXIV prohibited payment of poll taxes or other taxes as a condition for voting in federal elections. Amendment XXVI lowered the age of voting rights to eighteen.

3. Which amendments **increased** the power of the federal government? (Changes that expanded federal authority, taxation, or representation at the expense of the states or individuals)

   Amendment XVIII greatly expanded the scope of federal authority over private and interstate commerce by establishing the authority to regulate, control and prohibit the manufacture and sale of alcoholic beverages.

4. Which amendments **decreased** the power of the federal government? (Changes that restrict federal authority, taxation, or representation to the benefit of the states or individuals)

   Amendment XXI repealed Prohibition. Amendment XVIII officially returned control of alcohol to the states. However, it did not reduce the expanded authority over interstate trade the federal government had acquired as a consequence of Prohibition. Amendment XXII limits presidents to two terms, so that no president becomes too powerful.

5. Of all 27 amendments, which is the most important in your opinion? Explain.

   Answers will vary. The students will have different opinions. However, a complete answer should include reference to a specific amendment and the reason, or justification, for why it is most important.

Lesson 17

Upholding the Constitution and Protecting Civil Rights

We the people are the rightful masters of both Congress and the courts, not to overthrow the Constitution, but to overthrow men who pervert the Constitution.
Abraham Lincoln, 1859

Compelling Question: Do you believe you have a duty—as a citizen of the United States of America—to understand and defend the Constitution?

Key Concepts:

1. A fundamental **attribute** of our constitutional republic—essential to its success—is that the government derives its authority and power from the people. Only the people can change the Constitution and only through the amendment process.

2. Many proposed solutions to provide a more just, fair, and safe society sound good at first, but we must be careful that they do not violate the rights protected by the Constitution, especially the Bill of Rights.

3. As citizens of the United States, we must be on the watch to protect our freedoms guaranteed by the Constitution and participate in all elections.

How the Constitution Fulfills the Vision of the Declaration of Independence

In 1887, the historian and moralist Lord Acton wrote, "Power tends to corrupt and absolute power corrupts absolutely." The Founders of our nation were aware that throughout history people have sought power over others. They declared independence from England in 1776 because King George III and the English Parliament had abused the colonists' inalienable rights. So, when the Founders wrote the Constitution in 1787, they included many safeguards to prevent any elected official or branch of government from having too much power or abusing power.

The law keeps the people in control of the government—but only if the people constantly safeguard the Constitution from being undermined. And the people can protect the Constitution only if they are well informed about what the safeguards are, how they work, and what each one protects.

Fundamental Attributes of Our Constitutional Republic

1. **Common law.** The Constitution follows the principles of **common law** instead of **civil law.** All laws and governmental rules throughout the nation must uphold the common law principle that the people's God-given natural rights are supreme. The government must serve the people. Under common law, judges must consider precedent based on prior court rulings when ruling on new cases. And defendants are assured of trial by a jury of peers. These safeguards are to ensure that people can depend on equal treatment under the law.

   The Founders rejected the principles of civil law because civil law is based on the idea that the people are to serve the government. The state makes the final legal decisions. **Magistrates** act as both judge and jury. In other words, one magistrate alone makes important decisions affecting other people. Citizens cannot rely on precedent to know whether they are following a law or breaking it.

2. **Consent of the Governed.** The Declaration of Independence changed the course of world history, including that Americans would *not* be ruled by a king. The 56 signers of the document agreed that "all men are created equal, that they are endowed by their Creator with certain unalienable Rights, that among these are Life, Liberty and the pursuit of Happiness . . . That to secure these rights, Governments are instituted among Men, deriving their just powers from the *consent of the governed.*" (Italics added.)

   The Founders declared that a government is not legitimate and cannot use state power unless the people first grant permission (through elections). Not since ancient Israel had there been anything but rule by kings, queens, dictators, pharaohs, monarchs, or oligarchs. The adoption of the Articles of Confederation, the Northwest Ordinance of 1787, and the Constitution of the United States of America established how citizens would be represented in the federal government and how elected officials would honor their consent, with protections of those in the minority.

3. **Separation of Powers.** If a government agency can make the laws, enforce them, and judge their legality, then it has the power to oppress the people. As explained in Sessions 8, 9, and 10, the Founders divided government authority into three separate branches to limit the opportunity for any branch to overwhelm the others. The Constitution gives each branch different responsibilities and just enough authority to fulfill them. The legislative branch makes laws, the executive branch implements and enforces them, and the judicial branch judges whether laws are constitutional.

   Discussion Question: Has Congress violated the principle of separation of powers by transferring legislative duties to bureaucrats in the executive branch?

Background: Article I, Section 1, of the Constitution states that "All legislative Powers herein granted shall be vested in a Congress of the United States, which shall consist of a Senate and House of Representatives." However, many scholars say that the executive branch and Congress have altered the separation of powers by creating numerous commissions and agencies in the executive branch and allowing them to create rules and regulations that have the full effect of laws.

The result is that bureaucrats (not legislators) create detailed regulations that may impose fines and, in some cases, imprisonment. In order to ensure separation of powers, many believe that bureaucratic regulations that impose fines or imprisonment should be subject to congressional approval.

4. **Checks and Balances.** The Constitution provides three branches of government so that each branch's power can be countered by the other two branches. For example, if the president oversteps his or her constitutional power, the Supreme Court can overrule the president's decision or action. The president can veto bills passed by Congress that he or she considers unconstitutional or unwise. Congress can override the president's veto by a two-thirds vote.

   So, there are also checks and balances within the legislative branch with its two houses of Congress—the House of Representatives and the Senate. Representatives in the House are motivated to be highly responsive to the people in their districts. Their terms are only two years, so if they want to be reelected, they must vote on bills according to the will of the majority of voters in their districts. Senators have terms of six years to allow them more independence than representatives. Senators balance the different interests of the states with greater focus on long-term interests of the nation as a whole. It is difficult to advance a bill through Congress. It must gain broad support. Both the House and the Senate have to pass the same bill by a majority vote for it to go to the U.S. president to sign into law or veto. (See "How Does a Bill Become a Law?" at the end of Session 8.) Some major congressional actions, however, require a supermajority two-thirds vote.

5. **States' Rights.** The Tenth Amendment safeguards against the federal concentration of power. The federal government has no powers other than those specifically granted to each of its three branches. The Constitution reserves all other powers to the states or to the people.

6. **Bill of Rights.** The Constitution's Bill of Rights protects both individuals and groups against abuse of power at every level of government. It spells out our freedoms of speech, religion, association, the right to bear arms, and so on. And it prohibits government from taking our freedoms away. The Bill of Rights was also adopted to protect the rights of all people so that the government cannot restrict their basic liberties. Bills must be passed by a majority vote in both houses and sent to the president for action. But no matter how large the majority, no law or other action should violate the constitutional rights of any citizen.

   Discussion Question: Are state governments violating the First Amendment's guarantee of freedom of assembly and religion when they establish lockdowns of businesses, churches, and social gatherings to protect citizens from a pandemic?

   Background: Health and safety concerns arise in society that often cause well-meaning people to disregard the rights to freedom of worship and assembly protected in the Bill of Rights. The COVID-19 pandemic has resulted in some state governors deciding on which businesses are "essential" and which are not, resulting in shutdowns decreed by one person. These controversial decisions challenge the First Amendment and deserve scrutiny by all citizens.

   In November 2020, the U.S. Supreme Court answered a challenge to freedom of religion in a court case with five justices voting "for" and four justices voting "against." Governor Andrew Cuomo of New York, by an executive order, had imposed limitations of 10 and 25 people in houses of worship based on which COVID zone the church or synagogue was located. He imposed the restriction as a way to reduce the spread of the COVID-19 virus. The Roman Catholic Diocese of Brooklyn and Agudath Israel of America filed for injunctive relief against Governor Cuomo to stop the restriction. The Supreme Court ordered a preliminary **injunction** against the State of New York, that "the loss of First Amendment freedoms" is irreparable harm as a matter of law.

Discussion Question: Is our government violating the Fourth Amendment with the Patriot Act?

Background: After the terrorist attacks on the World Trade Center and the Pentagon in 2001, Congress approved universal surveillance by the National Security Agency (NSA). The Patriot Act allowed for collection of some personal information transmitted electronically by all citizens *without* a warrant or showing probable cause of the commitment of a crime. This has been challenged successfully in courts since then, just as the Founders would have hoped. A 2015 decision from the New York-based Second U.S. Circuit Court of Appeals said that collection of information relevant to terrorism does *not* warrant mass surveillance of phone records. Then, on September 2, 2020, the U.S. Court of Appeals for the Ninth Circuit (San Francisco) ruled that the mass surveillance of Americans is unlawful. The ruling determined that the warrantless telephone tapping secretly collecting data from millions of Americans' phone records violated the Foreign Intelligence Surveillance Act (FISA) and exceeded the scope of congressional power.

These are examples of how our judicial system is doing its job to check the power of Congress. Note, however, that those trying to protect America from terrorism say that "mass surveillance" wrongly suggests that the billions of calls and texts that occur every day are carefully monitored. In fact, the NSA equipment searches for patterns of words that suggest violent attacks, which would trigger a review, and the government cannot possibly monitor all citizens. It can only use the broad surveillance of metadata to suggest further investigation. This screening process can be used to extract the necessary data to show "probable cause" to a judge, who can then issue a warrant.

Discussion Question: Is legislation previously passed by Congress permitting seizure of physical property without due process a violation of the Fourth and Eighth Amendments?

Background: In 1970, Congress passed the Comprehensive Drug Abuse and Control Act, the first of several civil asset forfeiture bills signed into law by the president. These laws were created to fight the "war on (illegal) drugs." They allow law enforcement officers to seize and keep citizens' property without obtaining warrants for probable cause or charging citizens with a crime. These laws allow law enforcement agencies to increase their revenues and pay for law enforcement. These laws also have provided major sources of funding for law enforcement agencies nationwide. In 2019, the U.S. Supreme Court overturned a lower court ruling that had resulted in the confiscation of a man's automobile. The ruling said that the Eighth Amendment's Excessive Fines Clause applies not just to the federal government but to the states as well. As a result, the lower court had to return the man's car in 2020. Justice was served by the Supreme Court ruling, with ramifications nationally, and more cases regarding the Fourth and Eighth Amendments are expected.

Safeguard against Tyranny by the Most Populous States—The Electoral College

The Electoral College is another important safeguard against tyranny by the majority. The Founders wanted to balance the powers of the states so that neither the densely populated states nor the less populated states would have too much power. But they wanted all states to have a voice in the election of the U.S. president. So, in Article II of the Constitution, the Founders established the Electoral College, a brilliant system for, electing the U.S. president and vice president in a way that preserves federalism (Session 9). When citizens vote for a candidate for president, their votes are counted, and the top vote-getter wins their state's popular vote. But winning the national popular vote does not necessarily mean he or she becomes president. The Founders established a safeguard with an interim step whereby the winners for president and vice president in each state are granted that state's electoral votes. The number of electors each state has is based on their state's number of members in the House of Representatives and Senate. Today, the two major political parties each select a slate of electors. The electors of the winning candidates' party in each state then meet at the state capitol to vote for their party's nominees for president and vice president.

States with a large population have more electors than smaller states. But the system protects the rights of smaller states because all states have two senators and at least one member of Congress. It prevents the most populated states, such as California, Texas, Florida, and New York, from controlling who is elected president. Without the Electoral College, candidates for president and vice president would have little incentive to listen to the concerns of voters in the rural or small states.

The Electoral College plays a vital role in our republican form of government. It avoids tyranny by the majority, protects the rights of minorities, preserves states' rights, and promotes a stable two-party system. It also promotes federalism by allowing both the states and federal government to participate in the election process.

Safeguard against Government Meddling in Free Markets

The Constitution keeps the government from undue meddling in the nation's economic markets. For example, it prohibits laws restricting interstate commerce—the buying and selling of products or services across state lines.

The Founders learned from history, including the lessons learned by the early colonists (Session 2), that free enterprise was key to the success of a nation. Further, they were informed by the Scottish economist Adam Smith's book *The Wealth of Nations*, published in 1776 (Session 3). Smith documented how free markets provide greater national wealth than markets run collectively or by monarchs or bureaucrats. People are more productive if they can keep the results of their individual efforts, directly benefitting from what they produce. However, if a person's production must go into a group's common storehouse, most people lose their motivation to work hard, and they produce less. The Founders repudiated such **collectivism**, an economic system in which everyone shares the product equally, but less is produced. Instead, they blessed America with an economic system that resulted in amazing abundance that we now call **capitalism.** Further, Thomas Jefferson asserted that the exercise of free trade is a natural right in *A Summary View of the Rights of British America in 1774.*

The most important incentive for increasing national wealth is the assurance that neither the government nor anyone else can confiscate people's capital. The Fourth and Fifth Amendments of the Bill of Rights give this assurance. The Fourth Amendment protects the rights of people "to be secure in their persons, houses, papers and effects" [also called property] "from unreasonable searches and seizures." The Fifth Amendment requires that "No person shall be . . . deprived of life, liberty, or property, without due process of law."

The Constitution protects private property, including the profits from **entrepreneurship** and investments in capital. This protection and relatively limited governmental interference in the nation's markets have transformed the United States from a minor nation to one of the wealthiest and most successful nations.

Balancing Wartime Threats and Civil Rights

The federal government has a constitutional duty to protect its citizens and military bases from foreign wars and terrorist attacks. It also has a constitutional duty to protect the civil rights of citizens, including during times of war and threat of attack, although temporary suspension of some rights may be necessary. In those times, Congress and the president have difficult decisions to make on how to balance preventing attacks and safeguarding liberties. Consider whether the U.S. government's decisions were warranted or unjust in the following two of the many examples:

Japanese American Internment Following Japan's Bombing of Pearl Harbor. On December 7, 1941, Japanese government fighter planes bombed the U.S. naval base at Pearl Harbor, Hawaii, killing more than 2,400 U.S. military personnel and destroying 21 U.S. ships and 188 aircraft. Congress then declared war on Japan and entered World War II. Americans were shocked by this attack and naturally feared more Japanese aggression. And they feared that Japanese Americans might be loyal to Japan, spy on U.S. military operations, and pose a threat to the United States.

This panic and anti-Japanese sentiment in the United States led President Roosevelt, in February 1942, to order Japanese American citizens and Japanese citizens in the United States to be forcibly removed from their homes and sent to prison camps called "Relocation Centers" or "**internment** camps." The rationale was to move them away from military bases on the West Coast to prevent espionage and security risks. The U.S. government, however, had no actual evidence of Japanese American disloyalty. (The governments of Canada and Mexico took similar actions, and Peru, Brazil, Chile, and Argentina removed their Japanese residents to the United States.)

The U.S. government transported approximately 120,000 Japanese Americans and citizens of Japan, living mostly on the West Coast, to ten internment camps in the U.S. interior. Conditions were meager. Each camp was like a town surrounded by barbed wire and guard towers.

From 1942 to 1946, when the last camp was closed, the U.S. government violated the internees' constitutional rights guaranteed by Amendments I (right to freedom of religion, free speech, and assembly); II (the right to bear arms); IV (protection from being searched and having property taken for no valid reason); V (protection against being deprived of life, liberty, or property without due process of the law and just compensation or held without indictment); VIII (protection against cruel and unusual punishment); and XIV (protection against being deprived of life, liberty, or property by any state and right of equal protection under the law).

The U.S. Supreme Court failed to rule on any of the lawsuits against the federal government for violating the constitutional rights of internees. Finally, in 1976, President Ford issued a proclamation: "We now know what we should have known then—not only was the evacuation wrong, but Japanese Americans were and are loyal Americans. I call upon the American people to affirm with me this American Promise—that we have learned from the tragedy of that long-ago experience forever to treasure liberty and justice for each individual American, and resolve that this kind of action shall never again be repeated."

In 1988, Congress passed the Civil Liberties Act, which issued a formal apology and awarded more than 80,000 Japanese American internment camp survivors $20,000 each in **reparations** to compensate them for the ordeals they suffered. Only those who were incarcerated due to the government's policy received reparations.

The U.S. Government's Response to al-Qaeda's 9-11 Attack. On September 11, 2001, nearly sixty years after the attack on Pearl Harbor, the Islamic terrorist group al-Qaeda from the Middle East hijacked four jets on suicide missions that destroyed the World Trade Center in New York City and part of the Pentagon. In addition, the hijacked United Airlines plane headed toward Washington, D.C., crashed in rural Pennsylvania because the brave crew and passengers fought the terrorists. It was the deadliest terrorist attack on American soil in U.S. history—and the deadliest in world history—killing 2,977 innocent people and 19 terrorists.

The scenes of destruction were frightening and the loss of life horrific, yet the mainstream media pleaded for Americans to remain calm and not target all Muslims because most were not extremists who hated America. Instead of rounding up Muslim Americans and sending them to internment camps, President Bush appealed to the American people and Congress to increase security, especially at airports and on airplanes.

Congress made major changes, including a comprehensive federal law called the "Patriot Act." The Transportation Security Administration (TSA), which was part of the act, changed airline travel radically, including what people could bring on planes and X-ray screening of passengers to ensure that they could not board airplanes with guns or explosives. The Patriot Act included several controversial provisions, extending the surveillance of Americans in the name of preventing future terrorist attacks. (See "Is our government violating the Fourth Amendment with the Patriot Act?" in this session.)

Toward a More Perfect Union in Race Relations

Even though the United States abolished slavery and amended the Constitution to provide civil rights to former slaves, racial prejudice and discrimination persisted.

Darwin's Theory of Evolution. A major cause of racial prejudice was the theory of evolution developed by the English naturalist Charles Darwin in On the Origin of Species by Means of Natural Selection or the Struggle for Preservation of the Favoured Races in the Struggle for Life, published in 1859. He believed that life began by random chance in a simple one-celled organism that evolved into higher life forms. He developed his thoughts on "Favoured Races" in The Descent of Man, published in 1871—not long after the Civil War in which thousands fought and died for the freedom of African Americans. In his book, Darwin applied his theory of natural selection to humans. He wrote that all nonwhite people, whom he called "savages," were inferior to whites—hence, white supremacy. Many in the scientific community promoted Darwin's false and harmful idea of "scientific" racism, claiming that whites were superior. These ideas, of course, spilled over into the general public and politics.

The Ku Klux Klan and Jim Crow Laws. In fact, the Ku Klux Klan (KKK) was founded in 1865 by white supremacists who hated African Americans, Jews, Catholics, and Muslims. The organization violently opposed the Republican Party, which was founded in 1854 to stop the spread of slavery into the territories. Efforts by the Republicans to empower former slaves in the Reconstruction of the South and thereafter were countered by KKK-led lynching (usually by hanging). According to the Tuskegee Institute, 4,743 people were lynched between 1882 and 1968 in the United States, including 3,446 African Americans and 1,297 whites.

Following the Reconstruction of the South, some state and local governments passed laws that hindered blacks' voting rights and segregated blacks from whites in housing, transportation, and commerce. These laws were known as "Jim Crow" (a derogatory term for blacks) laws. In many parts of the United States, blacks and other minorities were discriminated against in housing, bank loans, employment, and educational opportunities.

Tulsa Race Massacre. Part of human nature has always been people's tendency to regard themselves as more important than others and to fear those who are different from themselves. An extreme example occurred in 1921 in Tulsa, Oklahoma. The Tulsa Race Massacre exemplifies the undercurrent of racism prevalent in the United States at that time. A supposed interaction of a black shoe shiner with a white elevator operator (both teenagers) sparked rumors and outrage in the white community, resulting in a white mob destroying 35 blocks of the Greenwood District in downtown Tulsa. Known as the "Black Wall Street," the Greenwood District was a thriving community owned predominantly by African Americans. On May 31 and June 1, 1921, the white mob attacked, and outnumbered armed blacks fought in self-defense to protect the accused black teen and their community. While only 26 blacks and 10 whites were confirmed dead, historians estimate the actual death toll to be as high as 300. Thousands were left homeless, and more than 1,250 homes in addition to buildings were burned and looted. An estimated 6,000 blacks were detained under armed guard at local fairgrounds for several days. Refusing to accept defeat, the black Tulsans rebuilt their houses and businesses in the aftermath of the massacre. All charges against the accused teenager were dropped.

The Tulsa Race Massacre was an ugly scene, an example of man's inhumanity to man, and it is a reminder of the evils of racism and mob violence. Yet, we must remember that we are all imperfect people who do not shed bad behavior easily nor change quickly.

Juneteenth National Holiday. Our nation has continued to grow in understanding and appreciating the history we all share as Americans. For example, on June 17, 2021, President Joe Biden signed into law a new national holiday to be celebrated every June 19th. It commemorates the day in 1865 when news of Abraham Lincoln's Emancipation Proclamation finally reached Galveston, Texas, and the freedom of all slaves was announced. "Juneteenth" has been celebrated in various parts of the United States since 1865. This federal holiday is the first new one since Martin Luther King Jr. Day was adopted in 1983.

Ideals of American Founding Documents. In summary, compare the ideals in the Declaration of Independence and the U.S. Constitution with the white supremacist ideas of Darwin, the KKK, the white mob in Tulsa, and all other racists. The Founders of our nation believed that all people are created equal and "endowed by their Creator with certain unalienable Rights, that among these are Life, Liberty and the pursuit of Happiness." They fought in the Revolutionary War and others fought in the Civil War for these ideals.

In his first inaugural address, President Abraham Lincoln quoted from the Preamble to the Constitution that "one of the declared objects for ordaining and establishing the Constitution was to form a more perfect Union." Lincoln recognized that the United States was definitely not perfect, that it never will be, and that citizens must constantly work to eliminate discrimination and make the nation more perfect. We all have a duty to uphold and protect our Constitution.

The United States of America was established on the vision of its Founders for a nation in which all citizens have the same individual rights and that these rights cannot be overruled by the government. These include the rights to life, liberty, and the pursuit of happiness. They also include equal standing of all citizens in the eyes of the law and equal opportunity for all citizens to pursue economic success.

At the time of America's founding, these ideals conflicted with the view that a king or queen had absolute divine rights (from God). That meant he or she had the power to tax, redistribute wealth, punish, or even kill, and local officials had little or no power to intervene. These conditions had persisted for centuries in every nation around the world. George Washington called America the "Great Experiment" because nations had previously been ruled by kings and queens, not by leaders elected by the people. How could it possibly work without a strong ruler deciding everything?

But history has shown that it does work, and the United States of America is a shining example. America has survived and thrived for more than 240 years despite its flaws, and it has done so because of the Founders' vision of freedom and the brilliant constitutional republic they gave us. They established a government based on respect for individual rights, coupled with ways to reverse bad laws and correct injustices. Over time, Americans have elected leaders with the integrity and compassion to make it a "more perfect union."

■ Key Terms

attribute. A quality or characteristic of a person, place, or thing.

capitalism. An economic and political system based on private property rights and in which a country's trade and industry are controlled by private owners rather than by the government.

civil law. A legal system in which governments (mainly in Europe and Louisiana) maintain that rights are granted by the government, not by God. Therefore, the government can take away any rights based on any justification it chooses. The United States operates under the common law worldview, but it uses the term *civil law* to refer to court cases between individuals or entities that often involve monetary settlements. (In contrast, criminal cases are brought to court by the government on behalf of the public against individuals or entities that break criminal law, often resulting in fines, imprisonment, or death.)

collectivism. In contrast to capitalism, an economic and political system in which a group or government controls production and distribution of goods and services.

common law. A legal system with the overarching philosophy of law which acknowledges that God grants all people natural rights (life, liberty, and property) and that these rights are not granted by government, yet the role of government is to protect these rights. The Founders established the United States government based on common law principles in the Declaration of Independence.

entrepreneurship. Setting up and managing business ventures and taking risks in the hope of making a profit.

injunction. A court order requiring a person to do or cease doing a specific action.

internment. The act of confining a person or people and restraining their liberty, usually as suspected enemy sympathizers, or for political reasons, especially during a war.

lynching. Mob violence, often by hanging, against a person suspected of committing a crime but who did not have a court trial, in violation of the U.S. Constitution. In the United States in the 1800s and early 1900s, white mobs often lynched black people, especially in the southern states.

magistrate. A civil officer or low-level judge who conducts a court or conference dealing with minor offenses or hears *preliminary* hearings for more serious ones.

originalist. One who interprets the Constitution closely to the original intentions of those who wrote it.

reparations. Payments or assistance to a person from a government to make up for damages, injuries, or injustices they suffered.

Additional Discussion Questions

1. What protects the people from abuse of their inalienable rights?

   The judicial branch protects the rights guaranteed by the Constitution when judges hear cases of abuse and rule in favor of those abused. Indirectly, if an elected official abuses the rights of the people, he or she can be replaced at the next election.

2. What protects the Constitution of the United States? What is an **"originalist"** when it refers to the philosophy of a judge or justice of the Supreme Court? Should judges be able to override laws based on their personal views?

   Judges must adhere to the original intent of the Framers of the Constitution and must make decisions based on the law and morality. An originalist is one who interprets the Constitution closely to the original intent of those who wrote it.

3. What is the danger of bureaucrats in the executive branch writing regulations that have the same force of law as legislation passed by Congress?

   Bureaucrats are not elected by the people. They are appointed as civil servants with many job-protecting laws. They often do not have adequate oversight and make rules (with the force of law, often including punishments) that go beyond legislative intent.

4. What happens when laws, including bureaucratic rules, become so voluminous and complex that even lawyers and elected officials can't understand them?

   Progress slows—sometimes even stops. When bureaucratic rules are vague or overbroad, those who want to do business hesitate to take regular business risks for fear of being fined or punished for their activities.

5. What is the danger of government agencies collecting and recording citizens' texts, emails, social media postings, financial information, records of transactions, and other personal information without first obtaining a warrant as required by the Fourth Amendment (Bill of Rights)?

   A judge must issue a warrant allowing the government to do such things based on "probable cause" that a person has committed a crime. A warrant is limited to investigation of the crime. Without a valid warrant, such collection of information is an "unreasonable search and seizure." It is prohibited by the Fourth Amendment. If this amendment is violated, the government demonstrates a tyrannical power over the citizen, and justice and freedom are in doubt.

6. How do the protections of private property provided by the Fourth and Fifth Amendments of the Constitution's Bill of Rights protect the productivity of America's economy?

   Without the protection against unreasonable searches and seizures of property, the government could seize citizens' goods or stop businesses from operating. This would have a ripple effect on other businesses that rely on them, thus hurting the entire economy. The Fifth Amendment prevents the government from taking private property for its use without "due process of law." This ensures a dependable and fair business environment so that law-abiding citizens and businesses will continue to be productive.

Lesson 18

Final Review, Part One

[I]f we think [the people are] not enlightened enough to exercise their controul with a wholsome discretion; the remedy is, not to take it from them, but to inform their discretion by education. This is the true corrective of abuses of constitutional power.

Thomas Jefferson

The Declaration of Independence states that all men are created equal. What did the Founders mean by this?

- While no two humans are the same, they possess the same natural rights.
- Even though there are rich people, poor people, white people, and people of color, they all have the rights to life, liberty, and property.
- While many people are in positions of power and leadership, none has a divine right to rule over anyone else.
- The Founders established the United States of America based on the principle that the people will elect their leaders and that there will be "consent of the governed."

What are the primary reasons we have a national government?

- To ensure that the natural rights of Americans are not violated.
- To protect the American people from invading armies and domestic terrorists who threaten the lives and property of Americans.
- To maintain the medium of exchange for buying and selling (coin money), facilitate communications (regulating telephone and other communication systems), maintain a nonpartisan post office system for delivery of the mail, and ensure free trade between businesses in the states.

Why did the colonies unite to fight the Revolutionary War against Great Britain?

- King George III imposed taxes on the colonists by decree without the consent of the governed.
- The colonists, who originally considered themselves Englishmen, were not treated the same as those living in England. They had no representation in Parliament as members of the House of Commons or the House of Lords.
- Great Britain increasingly countered the colonial legislatures.
- Not only did the English king refuse to address the concerns of the colonists, he added taxes, he denied them proper treatment before the law, and he ordered English soldiers to live in the colonists' homes.
- The list of abuses continued to grow until the colonists declared themselves independent from Great Britain and fought the Revolutionary War to secure their independence.

What are the Organic Laws of the United States of America?

- The Organic Laws of the United States of America are the four laws on which the United States was founded. They are also known as the "Founding Documents."
- They are:
  - The Declaration of Independence, July 4, 1776
  - The Articles of Confederation, November 15, 1777
  - The Northwest Ordinance, July 13, 1787
  - The Constitution of the United States of America, September 17, 1787 (Bill of Rights, 1789)

What is the relationship between the Declaration of Independence and the Constitution?

- The Declaration of Independence is the foundation, and the Constitution is the implementation of it.
- The Constitution is the charter that enshrines the principles in the Declaration of Independence.

Why did the Founders choose a republican form of government?

- The Founders rejected a monarchy, an aristocracy, and a direct democracy for the United States. As students of history, they knew how monarchs and nobility had abused the rights of commoners for centuries. They chose a constitutional republic rather than a direct democracy because they were aware of the abuses the ancient Athenian democracy inflicted on its citizens.

- The Founders did not trust a democracy's majority to protect individual liberty. They knew that democracy at its worst would result in mob rule.

- The Constitution provides a republican form of government as the best system to protect against abuse of government power and violation of the rights of minorities.

- The people elect representatives, senators, and the president and vice president to make decisions in government institutions that reflect their values.

- They designed the government with separation of powers, elected officials to represent the people, and the rule of law.

Why did the Founders replace the Articles of Confederation with the U.S. Constitution?

- The Articles of Confederation was too weak, and it could not fulfill the needs of a national government.

- After eight years under the Articles of Confederation, it became obvious that a stronger federal government was needed to effectively unite the states and provide for national security.

- Rather than a loosely united collection of states, the United States of America would have three branches capable of performing the essential national tasks of government, including a strong executive (president), with checks and balances to prevent any one branch from becoming too powerful.

- The Founders wrote the Constitution so that it would not go into effect unless it was ratified by three-fourths of the states since "consent of the governed" was critical for recognition as the legitimate government of the people.

What is the Northwest Ordinance of 1787, and why is it important?

- Although it is the least known of the four Organic Laws, the Northwest Ordinance was one of the most important laws passed by the government under the Articles of Confederation.

- Most of the Founders did not want slavery to continue, and they set precedent by prohibiting slavery in the Northwest Territory (now the area of Ohio, Michigan, Indiana, Illinois, Wisconsin, and part of Minnesota).

- The Northwest Ordinance demonstrated the priorities and beliefs of the American Founders: the importance of education, religion, and morality and that slavery was an evil whose spread needed to be stopped.

The Founders designed the law-making (legislative) branch of our government so that it would not be easy to pass laws. Why?

- If it were easy to make laws, there would not be enough discussion of the pros and cons of a law before passing the legislation. Without sufficient deliberation, the passions of the majority might overwhelm the concerns of the minority.

- Higher quality legislation is produced through purposeful and deliberate debate, not when laws and regulations are passed in the heat of political turmoil.

- The measured and unhurried pace of the legislative branch, especially the Senate, ensures a thoughtful process that considers the costs (including money and freedom) before making laws that affect our citizens.

- A robust exchange between opposing parties (and interests) allows for passing better laws that align with the U.S. Constitution.

Some of the Founders had slaves? Were they hypocrites?

- Although many of the Founders owned slaves, slavery was commonplace throughout the world during America's colonial era. In fact, slavery was an established institution that had existed throughout the world for more than 5,000 years.

- Letters and documents confirm that most of the Founders wanted to eliminate slavery when the Declaration of Independence and U.S. Constitution were written, but they saw no way to unite the southern colonies (which depended on slavery) with the northern colonies unless they compromised on the issue of slavery.

- The most important factor was that the Founders concluded they could not win the Revolutionary War against Great Britain unless all 13 colonies united. While many Southerners relied on slave labor to raise crops, the attitude and culture about slavery changed over time. As the culture changed, most people came to view slavery as incompatible with the laws of nature and nature's God.

- A major step taken by the Founders to eliminate slavery was to stop the spread of slavery into the Northwest Territories (Section XIV, Article 6, of the Northwest Ordinance). This meant there would be no slavery allowed in the future states of Ohio, Michigan, Indiana, Illinois, Wisconsin, and Minnesota.

- More than 600,000 died in the Civil War between the North and South to end slavery, resulting in the ratification of the Thirteenth Amendment in 1865.

Lesson 19

Final Review, Part Two, and the Duties of a Good Citizen

Let each citizen remember at the moment he is offering his vote that he is not making a present or a compliment to please an individual—or at least that he ought not so to do; but that he is executing one of the most solemn trusts in human society for which he is accountable to God and his country.

Samuel Adams

What is meant by "enumerated powers" in the Constitution?

- The Founders set up three branches of the federal government and specified their roles: 1) making laws through the legislative branch; (2) executing (carrying out) the laws through the executive branch (president); and (3) interpreting the laws to make sure they adhere to the Constitution through the judicial branch (courts).

- The Founders wanted to restrict the power of the lawmakers and limit what they could do so that Congress would not have unlimited power. So, they listed (enumerated) the powers allowed in Article I, Section 8, of the U.S. Constitution.

Why is federalism important?

- The thirteen original colonies (later, the states) had diverse interests. While they agreed to unite to fight Great Britain and protect the United States, they wanted to make their own decisions and govern themselves in most matters.
- Federalism refers to dividing power between the federal government and the state and local governments.
- The Founders wrote the U.S. Constitution to create a limited national government to secure the natural rights of citizens.
- Federalism protects the states from being overwhelmed by the national government so that issues affecting people in one state, for example, are decided by the people in that state.

What is the meaning of *states' rights*?

- Only people have rights. But the powers not granted to the federal government in the Constitution are reserved to states and individuals.
- Article VI states that the Constitution "shall be the supreme Law of the Land." The Constitution supersedes all laws passed by lower-level governments. Federal laws and treaties also must not conflict with the Constitution.
- According to the Founders, however, the federal governments' authority is to be limited to those powers granted in the Constitution.

How does our system of three branches of government—with each branch checking the actions of the others—protect our rights?

- Each of the three branches of government (legislative, executive, and judicial) can challenge decisions made by the other branches so that no branch has too much power. No branch can rule like a king. Each branch has to answer to the others and ultimately to the people.

- The legislative branch includes the House of Representatives with two-year terms and districts based on population (so that they are very responsive to the people) and two Senators from each state with six-year terms (so that they represent the whole state and take a longer-range view).

- We have the right and opportunity to present issues to members of Congress and to urge them to pass or reject bills in Congress. We can also seek assistance from our members of Congress regarding the protection of our individual rights.

- The legislative branch protects the rights of citizens by providing a way to pass new laws that correct injustices. The executive branch protects citizens from foreign and domestic attacks, and it provides enforcement of federal laws that protect them. The judicial branch protects citizens by ensuring that laws are constitutional and that the force of government cannot be used to harm individuals in violation of their God-given rights, including those enumerated in the Bill of Rights.

Why isn't the president elected by a simple national vote?

- The Electoral College (Article II of the Constitution; see Session 9) was intended as a protection of the rights of citizens in areas of the country that did not have the same population density as urban areas.

- Since the actual election of the president would be based on the established representation of each state in Congress, candidates for the office must campaign in both urban and rural communities in multiple states instead of concentrating on the most densely populated areas. In other words, all the country is important—not just the most populous areas.

- This can be seen as a protection of the rights of a minority in the face of the might of a majority. This was a key concern of the Founders in not establishing the American government as a direct democracy.

LESSON NINETEEN | 173

How should the judicial branch interpret the meaning of the Constitution?

- The Founders anticipated the United States growing larger and the need to consider different values and interests held by citizens in a diverse country. Yet they knew that the primary duty of the government was to secure the natural rights of all and that the judicial system of courts must be ever watchful of the Congress and president.

- The theme underlying the Founding Documents (Organic Laws of the United States) is that government by the people and for the people can survive only if the principles are upheld by interpreting laws as originally written.

- Judges should apply the original meaning of the Constitution and should not merely make determinations based on their own political preferences.

- We the people must elect only those who uphold the Constitution; Congress must pass laws that are constitutional; and the president must veto bills that are unconstitutional.

- The Constitution empowers the judicial branch to correct bad policies and laws by ruling them unconstitutional.

Why must we constantly uphold freedom and update the Constitution using the amendment process when necessary?

- Since the adoption of the Constitution, many corrections have been made to long-held views and bad laws that violated the natural rights of our people.

- A prime example was slavery, which was not eradicated until the Civil War and adoption of the 13th Amendment and the 14th Amendment, which extended the rights of citizenship to former slaves. Another example was the 19th Amendment, which gave women the same voting rights as men. The 26th Amendment extended voting rights to those 18 and older. (See Sessions 15 and 16 for further discussion.)

- The Founders knew that they couldn't foresee the future, so they provided the amendment process (Article V of the Constitution; see Session 10) to meet future needs. But they did not make it an easy process because the interests of all stakeholders need to be represented and the changes must be carefully deliberated.

- The Constitution requires that amendments be made only by a specific and difficult procedure, with considerable control of the outcome given to the states because state legislators are closer to the people than the federal government is. Article V requires a supermajority of three-fourths of the states to ratify any amendments before they become federal law.

- More than 11,000 amendments have been proposed, but only 27 have been adopted. The Founders understood that the amendment process is the safest way to make changes to the Constitution and that the rights and freedoms of the people must be protected by using this method.

Besides voting, what are the duties of a good citizen (18 and older)?

- The future of the country depends on each new generation to uphold our wonderful inherited freedoms and to work for a "more perfect union."
- The Founders warned that "We the People" must be vigilant in protecting the Constitution because there would always be those who want to change it for their own benefit or advantage.
- They recognized that people risk becoming subject to tyranny unless they are good citizens and pay attention to what's going on.
  - Attending local and state government meetings and testifying in opposition to bills contrary to the Constitution.
  - Speaking in favor of bills that support the Constitution.
- Citizens are responsible for electing accountable, intelligent, and virtuous people to public office. This includes (but is not limited to):
  - Keeping informed by reading and learning about issues.
  - Seeking out media (television, the Internet, and magazines) that present various points of view (both sides of the debate).
  - Thinking critically about the motives of those who want to change existing laws or add new ones.
  - Always remembering why the Founders established the Constitution's amendment process as the best way to change laws and uphold freedom.
- Citizens must hold elected representatives accountable for how they perform their duties and ensure that they support the Constitution.

What is the danger of a population becoming so uninformed that the citizens routinely elect legislators who pass laws that violate the Constitution?

If citizens do not know about the principles on which the United States of America was founded, or about the founding documents of the country, they will elect the most popular legislators who promise them more public programs and government spending. They will elect members of Congress and other officials who promote, for example, self-serving programs that favor themselves (such as "tax the rich people" or "give me free tuition"). They will do this without regard to the constitutional restrictions on the government. Further, if most citizens are not moral and the majority of legislators abandon the Constitution, the rights of minorities (whether rich, poor, people of color, or white) will not be protected.

Lesson 20

FREEDOMCIVICS® Final Exam

The FreedomCivics course has been designed to culminate with a final exam as Lesson 20. Please contact Freedom Education Foundation for a free bank of test questions (and answers) by emailing info@freedomeducation.org.

www.FreedomCivics.org

INDEX

A

abolitionist, 143
Adams, John, 15, 23, 30, 37, 40, 68, 106
Adams, John Quincy, 20
Adams, Samuel, 15, 37, 51, 68, 114
al-Qaeda attack, 159
amendment process, 100-101, 103, (174)
Amendment I, 127, 131, 158
Amendment II, 127-128, 134, 158
Amendment III, 128, 131
Amendment IV, 128, 131, 158
Amendment V, 128-129, 158
Amendment VI, 129, 132
Amendment VII, 129, 132
Amendment VIII, 129, 132
Amendment IX, 132-136
Amendment X, 132-136
Amendment XI, 140, 144
Amendment XII, 140, 144
Amendment XIII, 24, 57, 58, 69, 141, 144, 174
Amendment XIV, 51, 141, 142, 144, 174
Amendment XIX, 146, 150
Amendment XV, 142, 144
Amendment XVI, 142-143, 144
Amendment XVII, 143, 144
Amendment XVIII, 145, 146, 147, 15
Amendment XX, 146, 150
Amendment XXI, 147, 151
Amendment XXII, 147-148, 150, 151
Amendment XXIII, 148, 150
Amendment XXIV, 148, 150
Amendment XXV, 149, 150
Amendment XXVI, 149, 150
Amendment XXVII, 145, 150
American Revolutionary War, 30, 40
An Inquiry into the Nature and Causes of the Wealth of Nations, 22
Anti-Federalists, 68, 111, 112, 114, 116, 126, 134, 135
Articles of Confederation, iv, vii, 2, 39, 40, 41, 44, 46, 53, 54, 55, 58, 59, 64, 68, 69, 72, 86, 87, 91, 93, 94, 95, 101, 111, 112, 115, 135, 154, 167, 168, 169

B

Bill of Rights, v, vii, 4, 20, 25, 42, 56, 58, 59, 68, 70, 71, 100, 115, 125, 126, 128, 130, 131, 133, 134, 135, 136, 137, 139, 140, 145, 153, 155, 157, 163, 173
Blackstone, William, 3, 20
Boston, Siege of, 29, 30
Boston Tea Party, 28, 29, 31, 33

Bradford, William, 13
branches of government, 86, 102, 105, 106, 107, 108, 116, 155, 173
Bunker Hill, Battle of, 29, 30

C

Camden, Battle of, 31
capitalism, 10, 23, 24, 157, 161
checks and balances, 3, 6, 87, 88, 102, 105, 108, 109, 111, 113, 126, 155, 168
Cicero, 3, 6
circuit courts (courts of appeal), 100
civil jury, 129, 130
civil law, 21, 154, 161
Civil War, 24, 141, 143, 159, 160, 170, 174
collectivism, 157, 161
commander in chief, 50, 62, 95, 96, 97, 98
common law, 61, 63, 128, 129, 130, 132, 154, 161
Compromise on Slavery, 24, 69
confederacy, 1, 39, 44, 46, 64
confederation, 40, 42, 44, 46, 47, 50, 68
Connecticut Compromise, 67, 69, 72
consent of the governed, vii, 2, 3, 5, 6, 7, 20, 34, 101, 113, 116, 135, 154, 165, 166, 168
Constitutional Convention, iv, 5, 55, 59, 68, 72, 94, 101, 111, 112, 114, 126
constitutional republic, 3, 4, 5, 6, 70, 71, 96, 109, 113, 161, 168
Continental Army, 27, 29, 30, 31, 40, 41, 112
Continental Congress, First, iv, vii, 19, 20, 21, 22, 23, 24, 29, 44, 113
Continental Congress, Second, iv, vii, 19, 20, 21, 22, 23, 24, 29, 40, 44, 94, 113
Cornwallis, General Charles, 27, 31
courts, circuit, 107
cruel and unusual punishment, 129, 158

D

Darwin, Charles, 159
Declaration of Independence, iv, vii, 2, 3, 5, 10, 22, 25, 29, 30, 37, 39, 40, 42, 44, 55, 56, 58, 59, 67, 70, 87, 90, 126, 137, 140, 154, 160, 161, 165, 167, 170, 182
De l'esprit des lois, 21
democracy, 3, 4, 5, 6, 96, 113, 114, 115, 116, 168, 173
Dred Scott decision, 141

E

East India Company, 28, 31, 33
Edwards, Jonathan, 4

Electoral College, 96, 97, 98, 140, 143, 144, 147, 157, 173, 182
English Bill of Rights, 4, 20, 21, 25
English Parliament, 4, 7, 128, 154
Enlightenment, Age of, 19
Enumerated Legislative Powers, 87
executive branch, 72, 88, 91, 93, 96, 97, 98, 101, 102, 106, 115, 116, 154, 155, 162, 171, 173

F

federalism, 96, 116, 133, 135, 136, 137, 138, 157, 172
Federalist versus Anti-Federalist debate, 68
Fifty-Six Signers of, 37
Fifty-Six Signers of the Declaration of Independence, 37
France, 20, 28, 30, 47
Franklin, Benjamin, 9, 30, 37, 40, 68, 84, 177
Freedom Education Foundation, ii, vi, vii, viii, 198
freedom of speech, 127, 131
freedom of the press, 127
Freedom Ordinance, 56
free enterprise, iii, vii, 10, 15, 157
French and Indian War, 28, 31

G

general welfare, promote the, 75, 78, 86, 87, 90, 108
George III, King, 2, 4, 21, 27, 28, 30, 106, 154, 166
Glorious Revolution, 4, 7, 19, 20
grand juries, 128
Great Awakening, 4
Great Compromise of, 69, 72
Greek Democracy, 3
Guilford Courthouse, Battle of, 31

H

Hamilton, Alexander, 68, 84, 93, 94, 99, 108, 112, 113, 114, 115, 134
Hancock, John, 15, 37, 51
Henry, Patrick, 27, 29, 68, 114
House of Representatives, 3, 5, 17, 67, 69, 72, 75, 77, 80, 85, 86, 88, 89, 90, 91, 96, 97, 107, 140, 147, 149, 155, 157, 173
How Does a Bill Become a Law?, 91, 94, 155

I

impeachment, 94, 97
indentured servanthood, 12
Indians, Native American, 24, 28
Intolerable Acts, 29, 31, 33
involuntary servitude, 56, 58, 60, 65, 141

J

Jamestown, Virginia, 10
Japanese American internment, 159
Jay, John, 68, 108, 112, 114, 115, 182
Jefferson, Thomas, 30, 37, 40, 55, 68, 107, 115, 125, 157, 165
Jim Crow Laws, 159
Judeo-Christian, 3, 23
judicial branch, 68, 72, 101, 102, 106, 154, 162, 171, 173, 174
Juneteenth National Holiday, 160

K

Kings Mountain, 31
Ku Klux Klan (KKK), 159

L

land claims of, 41, 59
legislative branch, 69, 85, 86, 87, 88, 90, 94, 95, 96, 97, 98, 101, 102, 106, 154, 155, 169, 171, 173
Lexington and Concord, Battles of, 15, 29, 30, 40
Lincoln, Abraham, 37, 39, 53, 56, 57, 84, 153, 160
Locke, John, 37, 39, 53, 56, 57, 84, 153, 160

M

Madison, James, 1, 67, 68, 72, 84, 105, 108, 111, 112, 114, 115, 125, 126, 127, 128, 133, 134, 182
Magna Carta, iii, 4, 7, 14, 127, 128, 129
Marshall, Chief Justice John, 85
Massachusetts Bay Colony, 13, 14, 15, 16, 17
Mayflower Compact, 12, 15, 17
Minutemen, 29, 31
Montesquieu Charles de, 21
Morris, Gouverneur, 68, 70, 84

N

naturalized citizen, 143
natural law, or law of nature, 5, 25
natural rights, 2, 4, 5, 6, 15, 19, 20, 23, 25, 27, 33, 55, 56, 60, 69, 106, 113, 126, 130, 135, 137, 154, 161, 165, 166, 172, 174
negative right, 134, 135, 137
New Jersey Plan, 69, 72
Newton, Isaac, 20
Northwest Ordinance of, iv, vii, 2, 24, 41, 42, 53, 55, 56, 58, 59, 73, 154

O

Organic (founding) Laws, 55

P

Patriot Act, 156, 159
Pilgrims, 12, 13, 57
Plymouth Colony, 12, 13, 17
Pocahontas, 11, 57
PREAMBLE, 75
president, 11, 31, 40, 41, 49, 56, 63, 86, 88, 89, 91, 93, 94, 95, 96, 97, 98, 100, 101, 103, 106, 107, 109, 113, 114, 115, 143, 144, 147, 148, 149, 150, 151, 155, 156, 157, 158, 168, 171, 173, 174
private property rights, 5, 19, 22, 24, 54, 71, 128, 161
prohibition, 146, 147, 150
Puritans, 1, 2, 14

R

Raleigh, Sir Walter, 10
Randolph, Edmund, 69, 70
ratification debates, 126
ratification of the U.S. Constitution, 140
Reconstruction, 142, 159, 160
religion, 12, 20, 23, 46, 56, 101, 127, 130, 131, 155, 158, 169
republic, 3, 4, 5, 6, 27, 70, 71, 96, 106, 109, 113, 127, 161, 168
Resources, 182
Revolutionary War, 2, 4, 21, 22, 29, 30, 31, 32, 40, 41, 55, 57, 112, 128, 160, 166, 170
right of assembly, 127
right to a jury trial in federal courts, 129
right to bear arms, 127, 128, 155, 158
Roanoke, Lost Colony of, 10
Rolfe, John, 4, 11, 13, 15, 20, 21, 23, 25, 30, 37, 40, 51, 57, 68, 70, 84, 85, 106, 108, 112, 114, 115, 116, 149, 182
Roman Republic, 3, 6, 7, 23, 127
rule of law, vii, 1, 22, 100, 105, 106, 108, 113, 168
Rush, Benjamin, 9, 19, 30, 37, 40, 68, 84, 177

S

Saratoga, Battle of, 29, 30, 31
Senate, 3, 5, 17, 67, 69, 72, 75, 76, 77, 80, 81, 83, 85, 86, 88, 90, 91, 95, 97, 100, 106, 107, 140, 143, 147, 149, 155, 157, 169
separation of powers, 3, 22, 26, 86, 105, 106, 108, 111, 113, 115, 126, 154, 155, 168
Sherman, Roger, 30, 37, 51, 68, 69, 72, 84
slavery, 3, 12, 14, 15, 24, 53, 54, 56, 57, 59, 60, 65, 67, 68, 69, 73, 140, 141, 142, 143, 144, 159, 169, 170
Smith, Adam An Inquiry into the Nature and Causes of the Wealth of Nations, 22
Smith, Captain John, 11, 57
Sons of Liberty, 28, 31
Stamp Act, 28
states' rights, 137, 157, 172
suffrage, 146, 150
Supremacy of the Constitution, 101
Supreme Court, 96, 99, 100, 102, 103, 107, 109, 115, 127, 129, 136, 141, 142, 145, 155, 156, 158, 162

T

tariff, 143
Thirteen Colonies, 18, 39, 40, 44
Treaty of Paris, 31, 41, 55
Trenton, Battle of, 29, 30, 31
Tulsa Race Massacre, 160
Two Treatises of Government, 21

U

Upholding the Constitution and Protecting Civil Rights, v

V

vesting clause, 86
Virginia Plan, 69, 70, 72
Virtue, Necessity for, 23

W

War of Independence, 24, 41, 56, 128
warrant, 128
Washington, George, 2, 4, 11, 21, 27, 28, 29, 30, 31, 37, 40, 41, 56, 67, 68, 70, 72, 84, 94, 106, 112, 114, 126, 128, 148, 154, 161, 166
Whitefield, George, 2, 4, 11, 21, 27, 28, 29, 30, 31, 37, 40, 41, 56, 67, 68, 70, 72, 84, 94, 106, 112, 114, 126, 128, 148, 154, 161, 166
Winthrop, John, 4, 11, 13, 15, 20, 21, 23, 25, 30, 37, 40, 51, 57, 68, 70, 84, 85, 106, 108, 112, 114, 115, 116, 149, 182

Y

Yorktown, Battle of, 27, 31, 41, 114

Appendix I - Resources

Allen, Michael, and Larry Schweikart. *A Patriot's History of the United States.* New York: Sentinel, Penguin, 2004.

Arnn, Larry P. *The Founders Key: The Divine and Natural Connection Between the Declaration and the Constitution and What We Risk by Losing It.* Nashville, TN: Thomas Nelson, 2012.

Dobski, Bernard. *America Is a Republic, Not a Democracy, First Principles No 80.* Washington, D.C.: Heritage Foundation, 2020.

Forte, David F., and Matthew Spalding, eds., *The Heritage Guide to the Constitution,* Washington, D.C.: Heritage Foundation, Regnery, 2005 and 2014.

Grabar, Mary. *Debunking Howard Zinn: Exposing the Fake History That Turned a Generation Against America.* Washington, D.C.: Regnery, 2019.

——— *Debunking the 1619 Project: Exposing the Plan to Divide America.* Washington, D.C.: Regnery, 2021.

Hamilton, Alexander, James Madison, and John Jay. *The Federalist Papers* (also, *The Federalist*). Several publications available.

Higginbotham, Don. *The War of American Independence: Military Attitudes, Policies, and Practice 1763–1789.* New York: Macmillan, 1971 and Boston, MA: Northeastern University Press, 1983.

Lipsky, Seth. *The Citizen's Constitution: An Annotated Guide.* New York: Basic Books, 2009.

McClay, Wilfred M. *Land of Hope: An Invitation to the Great American Story.* New York: Encounter Books, 2019.

Skousen, W. Cleon. *The Making of America: The Substance and Meaning of the Constitution.* Malta, ID: National Center for Constitutional Studies, 1985.

Spalding, Matthew. *A Citizen's Introduction to the Declaration of Independence and the Constitution.* Washington, D.C.: Heritage Foundation, 2010.

Taylor, M. A., Trent England, and Jonathan Small. "Safeguard: An Electoral College Story." 76-minute documentary. New Salem, MA: Lightspeed Pictures, 2020.

We Still Hold These Truths: Rediscovering Our Principles, Reclaiming Our Future. Wilmington, DE: Intercollegiate Studies Institute, 2009.

Online Resources:
- Encyclopedia Britannica. https://www.britannica.com
- Foundation for Economic Education. https://fee.org/
- History. https://history.com
- National Archives Founding Documents. https://www.archives.gov/founding-docs

www.ingramcontent.com/pod-product-compliance
Lightning Source LLC
LaVergne TN
LVHW070530070526
838199LV00075B/6747